The Joyous Science

The Joyous Science: Selected Poems of Maxim Amelin

Translated from the Russian
by Derek Mong & Anne O. Fisher

White Pine Press / Buffalo, New York

White Pine Press
P.O. Box 236, Buffalo, NY 14201
www.whitepine.org

Publication of this book was made possible, in part, by public funds from the New York State Council on the Arts, a State Agency; the Institut Perevoda and the Amazon Literary Partnership.

Cover design by Robin E. Vuchnich
Cover image by Alberto Seveso, from his series *Heavy Metals*

Printed and bound in the United States of America.

Library of Congress Control Number: 2017956280

ISBN 978-1-945680-19-9

Contents

III.

IV.

V.

INTRODUCTION

The Joyous Science: Selected Poems of Maxim Amelin

If Mayakovsky wanted to "throw the classics off the ship of modernity," then Maxim Amelin wants "to throw modernity off the ship of eternity" (Dmitry Bak). Amelin is a loving collector of 18th century neologisms and a devoted student of Revolutionary word-smithing; he has been called an "archaist innovator" (Tetyana Bek) and compared to Nikolay Leskov's legendary Lefty—the fictional blacksmith skilled enough to make steel fleas *and* shoe them (Andrey Nemzer). Amelin's interests span centuries; he sails many waters, but his ship is uniquely his own. He explores 20th century ephemera in elegant, Latinate syntax. A "TV's aquarium" seduces him ("There's no peace on earth or in heaven"), but so do the uncut pages of antique books ("On the Acquisition of a Volume of V. I. Maikov's Works and Translations"). This is poetry that thrives on a tension of opposites, and *The Joyous Science* makes that tension available to English readers for the first time.

Maxim Amelin was born in 1970 in Kursk, a Russian city with its own set of opposites: it's known both for the local nightingales' distinctive song and for a bloody WWII tank battle. Amelin has devoted his career to publishing. In the 1990s, he co-founded the St. Petersburg house Symposium; today he is the editor-in-chief of OGI. In both capacities, he has worked to bring 300 years of Russian letters back into print. This manifests itself in his poetry, which is like a literary salon where the backlist comes to life. He is hypertextual and hyper-quotational. Books spill from every surface in his Moscow apartment. His kitchen is cramped, but the source of great meals. The author of three books of poetry, a selected works, and three translated volumes, he has himself been translated into over a dozen languages. Twice now he's visited the United States.

To track Amelin's significance in Russia, we need only follow his prizes. Since his debut collection, *Cold Odes* (*Холодные оды*) appeared in 1996, he has won the Noyvi Mir Prize (1998, 2015), the Anti-Booker (1998), the Anthologia Poetry Prize (2004), and two Moscow Reckoning Awards (2004, 2012). Many others have followed. In 2013, he received the prestigious Solzhenitsyn Prize for enlarging the "boundaries and possibilities of lyric poetry." The Poet Prize came in 2017. Both prizes are essentially lifetime achievement awards; for both, Amelin was the youngest poet so honored. What has caused this avalanche of accolades?

For many, it's Amelin's love of Russian and his explorations of its linguistic heritage. This interest, in turn, has much to do with when he arrived on the literary scene. Amelin is among the last generation of poets to grow up in the Soviet Union—he turned 21 in 1991—meaning that he entered his maturity amid a melee of new voices, styles, and schools. At the time Russian was in a state of flux. The U.S.S.R. had collapsed; new words poured in. This accounts, at least in part, for Amelin's interest in transitional figures. As a translator and classicist, he favors Catullus over Horace, for Catullus, he tells us, lived "when many things were being said for the first time." Ditto the *tridtsatiletnye*, or "Thirty-Year-Olds," Amelin's literary cohort. It matters, he insists, whether you're one of the "witnesses / to monumental times" ("Belated Ode to Catherine the Great").

If Amelin's style straddles centuries, his thematic concerns can also be split into a series of categorical opposites. Like John Donne, he mixes lyrical appeals to the Almighty with celebrations of bodily appetites. "Teach me to beseech you, O Lord," he opens one poem, "so my heart's hot lamp and frostbitten hide / might collide," while elsewhere he urges the reader to "unload your larder" and feast ("Satiety prevails, not taste"). He writes playful odes and political critiques. "[Y]our pediment," he tells Mayakovsky's statue, "shines with streams of sacrificial / urine." An unnamed state in "Fire-breathing beast" feasts on blood. Is it Putin's Russia? The U.S.? Puzzle poems alternate with crystal-clear elegies. Ekphrasis alone is unifying. His attention to statuary makes Moscow briefly feel like the Third Rome it long claimed to be.

Heaven and the undead constitute another tantalizing pair. Is the hereafter, he asks, like tumbling out of bed (see "Rising at morning from my graveside") or a rejuvenating sweat (see "Inscription over the Entrance to a Tbilisi Banya")? Is it a zombie apocalypse? In "Katabasia for St. Thomas Week," the "dead rise willy-nilly" and move "like snowstorms or squalls." In his futuristic ideas on human life and afterlife, known as the "Philosophy of the Common Task," Nikolay Fedorov proposes a theory of resurrection that's tied to our physical bodies. This idea fascinates Amelin; it is, he says, the "only original philosophical concept born on Russian soil." Its influence is everywhere in *The Joyous Science*, and it helps Amelin ask a question pertinent to us all: is salvation really worth it if the flesh can't come along?

Whatever the answer, Amelin is certain of one thing: a finished poem is its own Second Coming. This isn't self-flattery, just subject matter. Amelin fixates on the *un*finished, whether theological or aesthetic, and many poems here comment on their own making. His "Katabasia" is a "pie / encrusted with mold." He grudges the two weeks he's spent on a lyric he dismisses as "flyspecked fruit" ("There's no peace on earth"). He asks, "[w]hy repeat ourselves?" in the wake of past poems; he claims "it's too late to be taught a new tongue" ("Aesop's Language"). His is a self-conscious and self-critical poetry, perpetually aware of its minority status in the republic of letters. He compares its decline to the summer nights in St. Petersburg: "hello! here you go!—pfft! / The poem fell to prose" ("These nights that won't wear out in July").

This grim pronouncement does not, of course, keep him from writing. At 48, Amelin is an influential mid-career poet, spurred on by the same specter that spurs many: his own death. It's a haunting he has faced for some time. "I'm thirty but feel three hundred," he starts one poem, playing the premature Nestor. This is both a joke about Russian men's notoriously short lifespan and an act of self-deprecation. But no matter how insurmountable the task or how inevitable his end, the poet stubbornly persists, seeing in verse something that "holds our questions' answers, and our hope" ("A many-throated, many-mawed, many-tongued rumble"). Still, he's not free of doubt. There is always the option, he reminds us, to "go numb" ("Rising at morning from my graveside"). In choosing to continue, he offers one of the most reliable paths through post-Soviet verse.

Regarding our translations: *The Joyous Science* is a book that reminded us—as Joanna Trzeciak writes—that "translation is the art of choosing one's regrets." Anne, who first cracked a Russian textbook in high school, is the Russian speaker and scholar. Her expertise is in Russian prose translation. Derek is a poet who has adapted Latin poems. At an early stage, we decided that we could not ignore the rich texture in Amelin's verse. His poems overflow with rhyme, puns, neologisms, meters, and periodicity. If Nabokov collected butterflies, Amelin collects Russian forms. How, though, to preserve such colorful specimens in English?

How indeed, when the philologist wants to manifest every last reference and connotation, while the poet insists that any poem in translation must stand on its own English feet? As collaborative translators, we often found ourselves in the position of the lyric speaker from "I'm thirty but feel three hundred:" "cleaved into two hostile halves," "faced with two good options." We ended up doing what all translation must: we approached each poem on its own terms.

The Joyous Science is a book that selectively chooses when and how to be formal. A glance at our meters proves as much. We translate Amelin into syllabics ("Dawn's rosy advent reddened the east," "I'm both enraptured and indignant"); free verse ("Each and every day, save weekends and holidays," "The hulking carcass of a dead orca"); accentuals ("Let's hurry"); and concrete form ("Belated Ode to Catherine the Great"). Sapphics, which Catullus brought to Latin, seemed appropriate for an ode to a satyr ("The Statue of Silenus in the Capitoline Museum in Rome"). Amelin uses seven different forms in the sequence "In Memory of East Prussia"; so does our translation, though the forms aren't the same.

Rhyme too appears throughout, though it's both true and not. We're referring to our end rhymes, which we often slant—"succumb"/"gloom," "fashioned"/"post-mortem's"—as well as our rhyme schemes. Likes Keats's famous odes, Amelin's ten-line stanzas turn on five rhymes (see "Classical Ode to V. V. Mayakovsky"). We'll manage four. In other, similar poems we'll adopt three. Nowhere is our flexible approach to form more apparent than the title poem, "The Joyous Science." Amelin's mock epic struts in a six-beat dactylic dolnik, inspired by an experimental trochaic hexameter developed by Vasily Trediakovsky (1703–1768). This meter, however, isn't viable in English, so—taking a cue from Amelin's glosses, which are inspired by Coleridge's "The Rime of the Ancient Mariner"—we set the poem in a loose ballad meter. The choice did what good form paradoxically does: it freed us to focus on other parts of the poem.

Still, Amelin's poetic texture derives from more than fixed forms. He is alliterative and allusive; his work benefits from oral recitation *and* prolonged study. Over the past centuries, he writes, Russian poetry has branched out like an ancient and overgrown tree: "it may be crooked and twisted, but it's too late to do anything about that." You must study both what nourishes the tree, and what the tree itself can sustain, he notes, lest you try to "graft broccoli onto a plum tree, or pineapple onto an aspen." His allusions and archaisms are his way of growing, however crookedly, from the trunk out. If their meaning isn't clear from context or Google, we provide a note. Our diction will occasionally ring old-fashioned, echoing the original, while a coinage on our part—"[i]n August the flies go buzzerk" ("In August the stars shoot through the night air")—might fill in for a Russian one. Like Amelin, we pun, play with sound, and toy with idioms.

This is part and parcel to translation's frustrating art, which is all the more frustrating when working with poetry. Amelin describes the act like so: "Well, let's say there's a marble cathedral built on a rocky island in the middle of the Aegean Sea in the fifth century BCE." The translator, he argues, must "build the exact same thing in the Russian north. It might seem that no matter how you try, you'll just end up with the wooden churches of Kizhi." Still, with a little luck, you might match the landscape. With a little work, you might approximate a spire. In *The Joyous Science* we did our damnedest to rebuild on rock.

Derek Mong and Anne O. Fisher

The translators would like to dedicate their work to their son:
Whitman Avery Mong

I.

* * *

Что повторяться? — Больше, чем надо,
сказано — сделано — спасено
от сокрушения и распада, —
спелое в землю легло зерно.

Всходы проклюнулись из-под спуда, —
их не сломили ни жар, ни хлад,
Бог сохранил от лихого люда,
толп насекомых и диких стад.

Враг за врагом — суета пустая,
ибо, со древа упав, листва
не истощается, нарастая, —
нет нощеденства без ликовства!

Пламя заставило литься воду,
влага сподвигнула жечь огонь,
а величавых созвездий ходу —
ни преткновения, ни погонь.

Мудрому сумерки по колено, —
им утверждаются без труда,
вновь из-под пепла восстав и брена,
все погребенные города.

2001

* * *

Why repeat ourselves? More than was called
for has been said, done, or rescued
from breakdown and downfall—
the ripe seed sleeps beneath the earth.

Shoots peep from soil into sunbeams;
neither heat nor hoarfrost crack
them. God guards each one from
the brigands—insect throngs, the wild flock.

Let foe follow foe, for all are earthly
vanity. The foliage that's fallen
down won't wither, it will redouble.
The sad vigil ends with morning's adulation!

A flame forced the water to run,
and moisture fanned the fire's spark,
but for the grand constellation now spun
there's no harrier or stumbling block.

On the penny-wise all pound words
are wasted. The buried cities they insist
will be reborn simply confirm
what we already know: Pompeii existed.

2001

*   *   *

В августе звезды сквозь воздух ночной
падают наземь одна за одной:
тесно в обителях неба, —
зеркалом вод обманув, заманив
ширью просторов и золотом нив,
не отпускает обратно

тяга земная — тугая сума.
В августе мухи слетают с ума
в неописуемом страхе
от приближающихся холодов.
В августе тот, кто еще не готов,
спешно ведет подготовку

к смерти, к ничтожеству, к небытию,
припоминая поденно свою
юность, и зрелость, и старость, —
им равномерно подвержен любой
возраст, упругие губы мольбой,
зрением глаз утруждая:

что там виднеется? дуб или клен? —
Тело изношено, дух утомлен,
разум на части расколот, —
целого больше из них не собрать.
Старая кончится скоро тетрадь,
новая скоро начнется.

В августе солнце затмилось, и сей
знак во вселенной губителен всей
переживающей твари,
только прожорливая саранча,
крыл и копыт оселками звуча,
видит немалую в этом

* * *

In August the stars shoot through the night air
to earth, one after the other.
        Heaven's cloisters are crowded.
The oceans' mirrors lure stars, each beckoned
by those open spaces, or by the golden
        soil still virgin—the earth's

pull stuffs them into its full purse.
In August the flies go buzzerk—
        surely they're fearful
of the nearly-here freezes.
In August the dawdlers finally increase
        their pace and make haste; they gird

themselves for death, obsolesence, or oblivion—
recalling, in day-long portions,
        adolescence, adulthood, and dotage—
to which each age is equally
subject. Their lips are laden with this entreaty,
        their eyes with this vision:

What's that I see there? An oak or a maple?
My body is wearied; my soul crippled.
        Reason was split up for spare parts.
Its pieces can't be rendered whole.
The old notebook's not yet full,
        the new one not yet begun.

In August the sun's disk is eclipsed, an omen
pernicious, the cosmos over, to Man.
        It concerns all Creation.
Only the gluttonous locust, who sounds
out his hooves and wings like whetstones,
        finds in it any profit

пользу. — Четыре неполных стопы
дактиля, парные рифмы тупы,
            каждая третья — сестрица
сводная и не похожа ничуть.
В августе гуще становится путь
            и аппетитнее млечный.

Не поворачивается язык
то, что пишу, обругать. — Я привык
            жить за троих или больше
с помощью Божьей. Пора — не пора:
«Кем бы ты был, если б умер вчера?» —
            сам у себя вопрошая,

сам отвечаю себе, что никем,
невразумительных автор поэм,
            путаных стихотворений.
В августе страшного нет ничего:
свой день рождения на Рождество
            встретить надеюсь тридцатый.

1999—2000

or use… but see how these lines—bad iambs!—
run incompletely, their end rhymes a dumb
        thudding, before a third
line—ugly step sister—slips in…
In August the starry Way thickens,
        more Milky, more sweet.

I can't twist my tongue
to scold my own writing. I'm living—
        praise the Lord—at least three lives
at once. Is my time up or not?
"Who would you be if your life stopped
        today?" I ask myself;

my self answers: *no one.*
Just the author of incorrigible poems,
        of some muddled epics.
There's nothing scary about August.
My birthday's on Christmas;
        I hope to reach thirty.

1999 – 2000

* * *

Мне тридцать лет, а кажется, что триста, —
испытанного за десятерых
не выразит отчетливо, речисто
и ловко мой шероховатый стих.

Косноязычен и тяжеловесен,
ветвями свет, корнями роя тьму, —
для разудалых не хватает песен
то ясности, то плавности ему.

На части я враждебные расколот, —
нет выбора, где обе хороши:
рассудка ли мертвящий душу холод,
рассудок ли мертвящий жар души?

Единство полуптицы — полузмея,
то снизу вверх мечусь, то сверху вниз,
летая плохо, ползать не умея,
не зная, что на воздухе повис.

Меня пригрела мачеха-столица,
а в Курске, точно в дантовском раю,
знакомые еще встречая лица,
я никого уже не узнаю.

Никто — меня. Глаза мои ослабли,
мир запечатлевая неземной, —
встаю в который раз на те же грабли,
не убранные в прошлой жизни мной.

2000—2002

* * *

I'm thirty but feel three hundred,
and this rough poetry can't express,
either ably or artfully, the ten men
who could equal my worldliness.

Lead-tongued and heavy-laden—
roots rutting darkness, its branches
raking light—my song
lacks a ballad's punch and polish.

I'm cleaved into two hostile halves,
I'm faced with two good options:
The soul's reason-killing blaze
or the soul-killing cold of reason?

I find I'm unified—half-snake, half-bird—
first I plunge from above, then soar
up from below. I traverse both earth
and sky unsurely, stuck here in midair.

My stepmother, the capital,
sheltered me, but it's Kursk where I know
faces I can no longer place, souls
like those in Dante's *Paradiso.*

Nobody knows me either. My sight's slipped
from years rendering the unworldly earth.
How often now have I tripped
on that rake I left out in a past life?

2000 – 2002

* * *

Научи молиться меня, о Боже,
чтобы в сердце жар и мороз по коже
в дрожь бросали, сталкиваясь, Тебе
и при свете дня и во мраке черном;
сделай, переплавив меня, покорным
некогда предписанной мне судьбе.

Без Тебя — колеблемы ветром трости —
человеки! — мякотью рыхлой кости
покровенны — зреющие плоды
упадать со древа бесшумно жизни,
лишь переливающиеся слизни,
что никчемной частью своей горды.

Я ж Тебе последовал безрассудно, —
в бурном море брега взыскуя, судно,
Боже! — простирая ко мне лучи,
будь безжалостным и несправедливым,
но преображенного чувств приливом
благодаречию научи.

1998

* * *

Teach me to beseech You, O Lord,
so my heart's hot lamp and frostbitten hide
might collide, unleashing me, sweat-damp,
toward You, be it high noon, gloaming, or gloom.
Having smelted me, be sure I succumb
to the fate with which I was stamped.

Without You we're wind-bent thinking reeds—
O people!—pulpy flesh that sheathes
decrepit bones, swelled fruit that tumbles
from the tree of life noiselessly—another
slug's nacreous trail, which glimmers
with pride for a lot in life that's worthless.

As for me, I followed You so imprudently,
like a vessel in search of shore while the sea's
still storming. O Lord, extend your sunbeams
to me—be unjust, be pitiless;
for the one transformed by a surge of sense
You've the gift of grateful speech. Teach me.

1998

* * *

Огромная туша мертвой косатки,
волнами выброшенная свирепыми,
на пустынном валяется берегу.

Лоснящийся бок июльскому солнцу
подставив, плотная и тяжелая,
она уже начала разлагаться и гнить.

Вскоре громада прежнюю форму
утратит, лишится былой упругости,
грузно потом осядет и оплывет.

Душный прогорклого жира запах
неуловимо, но властно тем временем
воздух окрестный вытеснит весь.

Наверно, недели, месяцы, годы
должны пройти, прежде чем жители
мест отдаленных голый остов найдут.

Они на мелкие части распилят
его, из костей вырежут украшения
и напишут на них о бренности бытия.

2010

* * *

The hulking carcass of a dead orca,
flung shoreward by the surf,
lies on an empty beach.

Its glistening side, thick and oily,
roils in the July sun.
Hide and all, it has begun to rot.

Soon this bulk will shed
its former shape, that tautness lost
as it sinks, distends.

The choking scent of rancid fat,
foul and ineffable, will all
but replace the surrounding air.

Weeks will pass, months or years
perhaps, before dwellers from distant climes
discover its bare skeleton.

They will saw it down to small
ornaments, then write on these white
shards about the frailty of living.

2010

Классическая ода В. В. Маяковскому

Зам. председателя Земшара!
вознагражден за гертруды,
ходи по лезвию пожара
и битому стеклу воды
свободно, без препон и пошлин,
иль стой на площади, опошлен,
в потеках жертвенной мочи, —
лишь в сумрачное время суток
кучкующихся проституток,
смотри, В. В., не потопчи.

Смотри, в слепящее рекламой
многоочитое табло
неосторожно, самый-самый!
ножищей в тысячу кило
не звездани, В. В., навылет,
а то напополам распилят
и переплавят на металл. —
Ломая молниями строчки,
о свежестиранной сорочке
и памятнике кто мечтал?

Ты, друг всего и вся на свете
и лучший враг всего и вся,
из тех апартаментов в эти
переливающегося,
ты, для горилл и павианов,
как вывернутый Жорж Иванов
для павианов и горилл,
поверивших, что солнце — люстра,
но, слава Богу, Заратустра
так никогда не говорил.

Classical Ode to V. V. Mayakovsky

Vice-Chairman of the Globosphere!
Your hero-works will long abide;
though oft you've walked the flame's bright edge
and paced the shattered water's tide,
it's time to shed impediments
and stand atop your pediment,
which shines with streams of sacrificial
urine. As usual, when dusk grows deep,
the hookers cluster at your feet.
Look here, V. V., they can't be trampled.

And look! Billboards and blinding rows
of flashing screens—those can't be trashed!
You'll have to stow your two-ton switchblade
when you go walking, for if you slash
one ad they'll saw you through the middle
and smelt you down for cheap scrap metal.
So don't screw up those monstrous posters.
Who dreamed of lines in laddered steps
and craved respect from lowest plebs
while always wearing laundered collars?

It's you, best friend of all creation,
and foremost fiend of all, or many;
you had no fixed accommodation,
maneuvering 'mid folks aplenty;
antithesis of that artiste—
himself no friend to apes or beasts
who think a lampshade is the sun—
the émigré, Georges Ivanov;
and thank the Lord you are both one-offs,
not Zarathustra's Overman.

В четырехстопном ямбе трудно
сложить сочувственную речь
тебе, как тонущее судно
от гибели предостеречь, —
ни славы нет, ни силы класса,
ни рябчика, ни ананаса...
Стань, кем ты не был, кем ты был,
останься, — старцем и подростком,
всех шумных улиц перекрестком
и жеребцом для всех кобыл!

1997—1998

It's difficult composing paeans
to you in four-beat lines of iambs,
just as it's hard to right the ship
of love that's so hellbent to wreck.
The working class is one big louse;
there's no more pineapples, no grouse.
Become the man you never were:
grow old, but stay tradition's scourge,
the crossroads where all streets converge,
the stallion mounting every mare!

1997 – 1998

* * *

амелин
как ты смеешь
писать стихи
после 11 сентября
А. Василевский

Каждый божий день, кроме выходных и праздничных,
когда без надобности особой смысла нет
из дому выдвигаться в сторону центра,
с невыносимым скрежетом, скрипом, сипом,
визгом и лязгом, царапающим и дерущим насквозь

барабанные перепонки, на сумасшедшей скорости
поезд подземный привычно проносит меня
мимо того самого места, между Автозаводской
и Павелецкой, где моего приятеля, не из близких,
тихого человека и семьянина, каких еще поискать,

собутыльника мирового и страстного книжника,
ни гроша не стяжавшего честным себе трудом,
Борю Гелибтера (помяни в молитвах имя его, живущий!)
разорвало в куски во время взрыва шестого
февраля две тыщи четвертого года от Рождества

Христова, в пятницу, в тридцать две минуты девятого,
едущего на работу в утренний час пик,
не подозревая, что ему, бедолаге, за пятьдесят четыре
дня до сорокатрехлетия в самое средоточье
угодить (о случайность бессмысленная!) суждено,

и приходят мне в голову то проклятия гневные:
«Тем, кто отдал не дрогнув страшный приказ, и тем,
кто, сознавая и ведая, что творит, исполнил,
пусть не будет покоя ни на том, ни на этом свете,
ни в холодных могилах, ни в жарких постелях телам

*   *   *

amelin
how dare you
write poems
after september 11
A. Vasilevsky

Each and every day, save weekends and holidays,
when there's no reason or special occasion
to leave my apartment and head downtown,
the same underground train—racing at insane speeds, its
unbearable rattling and grinding, screeching

and shrieking, clanging and clawing that's fit
to flay my eardrums to the bone—carries us past
the exact spot between two stations, Avtozavodskaya
and Paveletskaya, where a friend, not my nearest
or dearest, but a quiet man and loving father,

the kind that's daily more endangered, always willing
to go drinking and a book-lover to boot,
the kind whose hard work never won him a penny,
Borya Geliebter (speak his name in your prayers, ye who live!),
was blown to bits in that explosion on the sixth

of February, in the two thousand and fourth year
of our Lord, on a Friday, at thirty-two minutes
past eight, as he was commuting in the morning
rush hour, without the slightest notion that he—
the poor guy, just fifty-four days shy

of his forty-third birthday—was slated to land
(oh senseless fate!) in tragedy's messy center; and then
a host of thoughts comes into my head, from furious
curses—"Let those who gave this sordid order,
and those who (aware of their actions) still acted,

их не спится, а душам готовится кара сугубая!» —
то смиренные мысли о том, что непостижим
человеческому разумению небесный промысел тайный
и к нему подступаться с мерой земной бесполезно,
что рождение смертных, жизнь и кончина в руках

у Творца, всех блаженных Своих обратно зовущего:
«Да пребудет благословен возлюбленный мной!» —
то предчувствия смутные, мол, если Общего дела
философ окажется прав и точнейших данных
для грядущего воскрешения понадобится цифирь,

можно будет ее почерпнуть отсюда, и в опровержение
горьких слов иного мыслителя доказать,
что поэзия после Освенцима и ГУЛАГа, кровавых
революций и войн, Хиросимы, Багдада, Нью-Йорка
может быть, но какой? — кто знает, — возможно, такой.

2004—2010

find no peace in this life or the next;
whether they rest in cold graves or hot beds may they
get no response, for a special retribution awaits their souls!"—
to humble thoughts of heaven's hidden works,
which reason can't fathom nor human dimensions measure,

since our births as men, our lives and ends,
reside in the Creator's hands, who always calls
his blessed back with "Blessed be those beloved to me!"—
to vague ruminations on things foreboding:
how, if the philosopher of the Common Task is correct

and the resurrection requires numerical data, here's where
you'll find it, thus proving (despite a certain thinker's bitter claim)
that after Auschwitz and the Gulag, after bloody wars
and revolutions, after Hiroshima, Baghdad and New York, there
can be poetry…
but what kind? Who's to say, maybe this kind right here.

2004 – 2010

* * *

Гул многоустый, многоязычный, многогортанный,
вширь раздаваясь, вглубь проникая, ввысь устремляясь,
души живущих ужасом полнит, страхом объемлет,
в трепет приводит всех от умерших до нерожденных:
что происходит? что исчезает? что возникает?

Вся во вселенной тварь ощущает плотью сквозною
проникновенный свет, исходящий из ниоткуда,
из неподвижной точки ничтожной, зоркому глазу
неразличимой в круговороте лиц и событий,
но и ответы в нем на вопросы есть и надежда.

2005—2010

* * *

A many-throated, many-mawed, many-tongued rumble
resounds, coming nigh, soaring high, casting wide,
to infuse each soul with horror, wrap it in fear like a shroud,
setting all, from the dead to the unborn, atremble:
What's happening? What's coming? What's gone?

And the cosmos's uncountable creatures now feel
a light on their transparent skin, transmitted
from an immutable mote, so tiny even a keen eye
can't pinpoint it in the maelstrom of faces and events—
but it holds our questions' answers, and our hope.

2005 – 2010

Изваяние Силена в Капитолийском музее в Риме

Ирине Ермаковой

Безымянного страж именитый сада,
бородатый, косматый, великорослый,
с переброшенной шкурою через рамо
кососаженное,

козлоногий, задастый, парнокопытный,
многогроздую между рогов кошницу
подпирающий шуйцей, в деснице свесив
кисть виноградную, —

что печаль по челу пролегла, Силене?
Мрачноличен зачем и понуровиден?
Ах, и кто же, скажи, не стыда, не срама, —
уда заветного,

прямотою прославленного стрекала
кто лишил-то тебя? За какие вины?
Неужели твои сочтены проказы
за преступления?

Позабыт-позаброшен толпой пугливых
прежде нимф, нагловатых насмешниц ныне, —
хоть гоняйся за ними, хоть не гоняйся,
всё одинаково,

ибо надо, поймавши, сражать, а нечем.
Потерявшему большее потерявшим
меньшее не наполнить обломком лона
влаготочивого, —

The Statue of Silenus in the Capitoline Museum in Rome

for Irina Yermakova

O famous guard before a nameless garden,
bearded, shaggy, hugely tall, with pelts that fall
over your enormous shoulders, much broader
    than an oxen's back,

goat-legged, big-butted, poised on cloven hooves,
on your head a basket rests between your horns,
your right hand on the handle, your left dangling
    a cluster of grapes.

Why does sadness strain your brow, O Silenus?
Why the gloomy visage and dejected mien?
Ah! Tell me! Who's the one who bluntly stripped you
    of what's neither shame

nor a sin but an appendage that's precious—
your exalted prick! Who? And to right what wrong?
Could any of your escapades really be
    considered a crime?

Spurned by a herd of formerly timid nymphs
and forgotten, whether you chase or disdain
to give chase and let those rude mockers remain—
    isn't it the same?

For after they're trapped, you'll have to do battle,
and what could you possibly bring to the fight?
You can't fill their wet laps with your stump—not in
    the least, not since you're

ни на что похотливый скопец не годен,
безоружный же муж никому не нужен,
оттого и поставлен в музее — Музам
на поругание.

2000

the one who's lost most. Lewd eunuchs are useless.
There's not a man who thinks to stand sans his blade.
And so you're dismissed to a museum, for
Muses to abuse.

2000

* * *

Раздерган Гомер на цитаты рекламных афиш:
по стенам расклеены свитки,
гексаметра каждый по воздуху мечется стиш
на шелковой шариком нитке, —

то долу падет, то подскочит горе. Не о том,
что лирой расстроенной взято, —
рожки придыханий о веке поют золотом,
где небо по-прежнему свято,

мечи не ржавеют от крови, курится очаг,
волам в черноземе копыта
приятно топить и купаться в лазурных лучах.
Но чаша страданий отпита

однажды навеки, — скорбе́й и печалей на дне
горючий и горький осадок,
железного века достойному пасынку, мне
да будет прохладен и сладок.

1992—1996

*   *   *

Homer's been shredded to quotes for the billboards:
        his scrolls unfurl and spread
to paper the walls, his hexameters bobbing—balloons
        we tied to silk threads—

the lines drop down a vale, then hop a mountain.
        Still the guttural "h," cued
by a curl, proves the song's provenance:
        the Golden Age. The lyre's still true.

Swords aren't rusting from gore, hearths keep smoking,
        and the ox bathing in sun's
azure still stomps the black earth with its hooves.
        But the ancient cup

of suffering was drunk and emptied for all time.
        Its burning, bitter dregs
of grief and woe will be sweet and cool to me,
        the Iron Age's worthy stepson.

1992 – 1996

* * *

Восстав от сна, взвожу на небо скромный взор;
Мой утренннюет дух правителю вселенной...
Г. Державин, “Евгению. Жизнь Званская”

По утрам, восстав как из гроба,
продираю глаза с трудом,
и расплывчато глядя в оба,
сам не зная, куда ведом,

в мысленной барахтаюсь каше,
полудрему и полуявь
разграничить силюсь, но чаши
весовые — то влевь, то вправь —

ни на миг не могут на месте
удержаться, — сквозь сновидень
глас трубы, запеченной в тесте,
внятно слышу, на Судный день

пробуждение — мню — похоже,
выбирая одно из двух —
онеметь, иль воскликнуть: «Боже!
мой Тебе утренню́ет дух».

2001—2003

*   *   *

Rising from slumber, I lift my humble gaze skyward;
I rouse my spirit to seek the universe's ruler...
Gavriil Derzhavin, "To Yevgeny. Life at Zvanka"

Rising at morning from my graveside,
I rub these eyelids till they're lucid,
and then, squinting windward,
I set off—unsure where I'm directed—

only to stumble through my thought's thicket.
Daily I strive to divide my half-dreams
from this half-light, but the cupped scales
dip—first to waking, then to fictions—

and won't hold still a whole second.
But through dream's doughy incubation
a trumpet, also baked in pastry, cries—
I clearly hear it, calling me to awaken.

I imagine it's the call to Judgment,
leaving me to choose between one of two
options: go numb or exclaim "My God!
I rouse my spirit to seek You."

2001 – 2003

* * *

Когда бы зрели мы и дух, как видим тело,
о как бы сердце в нас тогда заледенело;
представилось тогда б очам, что в смутной мгле
с толпою мертвецов мы бродим по земле!

Из церковного календаря за 1845-й год
(цитирую по памяти)

«Ни на земле, ни в небе нет покоя,
и мертвые выходят из могил
в обновах модных одного покроя
теснить живых, — загробный свет не мил:
то холодно, насколько мне известно,
то душно им, то страшно там, то тесно,

как мне когда-то в Питере. Но я
в завидном положении живого:
не к спеху мне и очередь моя
не подошла до — как его? — Ростова
один купейный покупать билет.
Меж выходцами выехавших нет,

иные проплывают мимо лица,
расчетливыми взорами горя, —
тепла в них нет, за них нельзя молиться.
Я с детства помню из календаря
церковного за прошлый век четыре
стиха про мертвецов, бродящих в мире

толпой бездушной, знаю наизусть.
Тела в роскошных пышные нарядах —
любовь и радость, ненависть и грусть, —
они не подпускают их и нá дух
без лишних слов и отгоняют прочь,
а в остальном такие же, точь-в-точь.»

*   *   *

If we beheld the soul as we see our own bodies,
O how the heart within us would freeze,
these eyes then would apprehend, through a dim gloom,
the dead gathered on earth, which together we'd roam.
From a church calendar, 1845
(quoting from memory)

"There's no peace on earth or in heaven,
and the dead disembark from their coffins,
bedecked in fresh outfits identically fashioned,
to squeeze out the living. Our post-mortem's
unkind, chilly sometimes, so far as I know—
or it's stuffy, a touch scary, and crowds overflow

as they did for me once in St. Petersburg. Still, I am
in the living's enviable situation:
in no mood to rush, and my turn's not come
up to buy a ticket—where to again?
Rostov!—for a four-seat compartment.
Among those newly departed many left

us incompletely, and still graze my face
with their calculating gaze. It burns,
though no warmth pervades them; we can't pray
for them. Since I was small I've recalled—from
a church calendar of the previous era—four
lines about corpses, wayfaring through nature

in spiritless crowds. I know them by heart.
Flesh is arrayed in lush and luxurious robes.
Love and gladness, sadness and hate—
it won't let these linger, not on your life, closed
off without a word lost, each feeling ushered
away. In all else we're mirrored, word-for-word."

Над этими стихами две недели,
конечно, с перерывами на сон,
на «Pierre Cardin»'а синего, на теле
(аквариум соблазна), «Paul Masson»,
на скромные пельмени с майонезом,
Наташу, на «Gilette» с одним порезом,

как минимум, я прокорпел, и вот —
какой ни есть — итог: не слишком ярок
и не засижен Музами сей плод.
Дороже выклянченный мне подарок
из Божьей шуйцы, чем неясно из
десницы чьей непрошеный сюрприз.

(Немного потеряв, немного выграв,
я позабыл одну простую вещь —
эпиграфу предпосланный эпиграф,
здесь в скобках — как бы ни был он зловещ —
его пишу, *помилуй, Боже!* («Имя
имаши, яко живъ, а мертвъ еси».) *мя.*)

1996—1999

At least two weeks on a single poem—
with brief pauses, of course, to lie down,
for a navy-blue Pierre Cardin, for that temptation
(TV's aquarium), for wine by Paul Masson,
or mayonnaise over humble *pelmeni,*
for Natasha and a Gilette razor with its lonely

blade—I've slaved. And see, here,
for better or worse, is the result: flyspecked fruit
that's less than Muse-bedecked, its luster
much reduced. But gifts I wheedle from God's left
hand are dearer by far than some token offered,
unasked for, in the right hand of the Lord.

(And with a smidgen won, a smidgen lapsed,
I momentarily miss one simple thought—
an epigraph is this epigraph's preface,
here parenthesized—no matter how sinister it
reads, I write it, *Lord have mercy* ["Thou hast a name
as if thou livest, but art dead"] *upon me.*)

1996 – 1999

II.

Веселая наука,
или
Подлинная повесть о знаменитом Брюсе, переложенная стихами со слов нескольких очевидцев

Ирине Поволоцкой

Всем о тебе поведать нужен настрой особый, —
Музы одной не хватит, даже девятки Муз
было бы маловато, но — собери попробуй —
разбрелись, разбежались, — удивительный Брюс! —

Не святой, не властитель, не разбойник, не воин, —
в чем же твои заслуги? — житие каково? —
кто же ты, что по праву вечности удостоен? —
Разве слепая жница — смерть — обошла кого? —

О! про тебя словечко молвить неосторожно
вслух, тем более повесть целую расписать
боязно, потому что и поплатиться можно
головой неразумной запросто. — Время! вспять

Вступление. — Сетования по поводу несвоевременной отлучки всех известных Муз. — Объявление имени главного героя. — Попытка определить его отличие от противного. — Осознание опасности для повествователя, могущей постигнуть его в продолжение повести. — Призвание времени.

двигнись. — Гнедую пару-тройку лихих столетий
запрягай-ка — да в Питер-бурх на Неве-реке
широкошумной. — Правит бал не второй, не третий
Петр: вся держава в правой, скипетр в левой руке,

Смелый приступ к предмету. — Парадный портрет Петра Первого. — Его тайные мысли.

на голове корона. — Весь — натюрморт, персоной
собственной восседает гордо на троне он,
туркам грозя и шведам пальцем, России сонной
перебить замышляя сладкотягучий сон.

The Joyous Science,
or
The True Story of the Famous Bruce, Composed in Verse from the Accounts of Several Eyewitnesses

for Irina Povolotskaya

A new mood I'll need to tell your tale,
and nine Muses are too few;
besides, they're chasing butterflies.
Behold stupendous Bruce!

No saint or king, no knight or thief,
how'd you reach our books?
Explain your claim to such renown.
You're one whom Death forsook!

I'm scared to let a loose word slip,
and scareder still to rhyme
your story. I'd pay for each mistake
with my poor neck. But Time—

Introduction. Complaint regarding the untimely truancy of the known Muses. The main character's name is announced. An attempt to determine the nature of his excellence. The narrator admits full cognizance of the danger that may threaten him in the course of the tale. An appeal to Time.

go back! Hitch up three hot-blooded
centuries till we meet
in Peter's city, down where the River
Neva murmurs. Let's greet

A bold approach to the subject at hand. Peter the Great's portrait in full parade dress. His secret thoughts.

that roost's new ruler: Peter the Great—
not First, Second, or Third—
whose right hand holds the orb, whose left
wields the scepter. He's our lord

crowned and handsome as a statue.
He threatens Turks and Swedes
with a wagging finger; he shakes Russia
from her slow, sweet sleep.

Служит ему исправно Брюс: например, погоды
все перемены знает в точности наперед,
предрекает по звездам всех сражений исходы, —
и без Брюса не ходит Петр ни в один поход:

Деловые и практические качества Брюса, проявленные им во время войны.

где там стоять пехоте, пушкам палить куда там. —
Надобно — остановит солнца по кругу бег,
может в глаза тумана напустить супостатам, —
средь июльского зноя вызвать январский снег, —

на море сделать бурю, — вражеский флот пожаром
испепелить внезапно, свергнув огонь с небес. —
Словом, Петру победы все доставались даром, —
с Брюсом у силы русской видимый перевес. —

А в промежутках между войнами Брюс орешки
грецкие знаний книжных не устает колоть,
наблюдая паденье яблок, орла и решки. —
То призывает разум, дабы душа и плоть

Мирные подвиги Брюса, его великие открытия: закон всемирного тяготения, теория вероятностей. — Философские размышления. — Астрономические наблюдения.

прение прекратили; то замирает перед
дальновидным подзором, острый вперяя взгляд
в россыпь созвездий вещих; то поминутно мерит,
заново размечая вечности циферблат,

время. — Но шумных пиршеств он не любил. — Однажды
гул ассамблеи пьяной, танцы для живота —
жарко! — «Воды бы! море, — умирая от жажды, —
выпил бы», — Брюса просит царь, — и пошла вода,

Презрение Брюса к необузданным удовольствиям знати. — Необычайный случай во время безудержного разгула, а именно: мнимое наводнение.

And Bruce is Peter's humble aid
in matters of the weather.
The stars tell him the battle's end,
he guides Peter's warfare:

The practical and efficient qualities that Bruce displays in war.

where troops should go, where to unloose
the salvos. He can stun
the sun's slow run; he can wrap mists
around his foe's vision.

In July he'll call up torrid snows,
or let a tempest crash
the shoreline; he'll rain his fire down
till ships smolder in ash.

In short, all Peter's victories
were given to him gratis;
With Bruce forever at his side
Russia held the advantage.

What time was left between the wars,
found Bruce cracking the books;
he'd track an apple's downward fall,
he marked how cast dies shook.

Bruce's peace-time accomplishments and great discoveries: the law of universal gravity, the theory of probability. Philosophical musings. Astronomical observations.

He reasoned that the soul and flesh—
or so he thought with bated
breath—might cease their strife; he charted
the stars constellated.

He even measured time's slow tick,
how clockfaces never cease.
Eternity's his minute plaything.
And yet he hated feasts.

Once, during one drunken romp
(belly-dancers, hellish heat)
the Tsar cried out to Bruce: "Water!
I could outdrink our fleet!"

Bruce scorns the elite's unfettered pleasures. An unusual event during the profligate revelry. To wit: an imaginary flood.

потекла водопадом с лестниц, по коридорам
бурным потоком, в щели пола и потолка, —
все закричали криком, все заорали ором:
«Из берегов гранитных вышла Нева-река!» —

«Наводнение!» — Гости испугались потопа,
дамы задрали юбки, на столы повскакав, —
срамотою зияет Азия и Европа. —
Вынул из пола пробку Брюс, засучив рукав,

вынул — и стало сухо. — Больно скучна потеха
царская: вот водою он возьми да ошпарь
всех ледяной, студеной, — содрогаясь от смеха,
заливается звонко. — Грозен и мрачен царь —

Неблагоприятное для Брюса последствие: ссора с Петром.

набок сползла корона. — К царскому взвилась уху
свита, — ох, не по нраву Брюсовы чудеса. —
«Вон из столицы новой в старую, чтобы духу...» —
Петр не успел домолвить. — За полтора часа

Вынужденный побег. — Путешествие из Петербурга в Москву. — Описание летательного устройства Брюса.

Брюс до Москвы добрался цел, невредим. — Вдогонок
кинулись — не догнали. — Ибо в запрошлый год
он из стальных и медных планок и шестеренок,
скреп и пружин составил аероветролет, —

And so the waves rushed through cracks
in floors and corridors.
"The Neva's burst its granite banks!"
the hordes (now deluged) roared.

"It's the Flood!" some drunk repeated.
Stairwells were waterfalls.
Ladies hiked their skirts and hopped—
their shame was virginal!—

upon the tables. So Bruce at last
rolled up his dry sleeves.
He pulled the cork from the floorboard.
The seas at last receded.

In contrast, Peter's performance bored.
He'd douse or scald his churls.
He'd play with water, shake with mirth...
But then turn mean and surly.

The consequences are inauspicious: a quarrel with Peter.

His crown had slid upon his head;
his court won't cease to blandish.
They whispered in his regal ear—
Bruce's powers are devilish!

And so the Tsar exclaimed, "Get out
of my new capital!
Go back to the old one!" His threat
was not rhetorical.

Forced to flee. The journey from Petersburg to Moscow. A description of Bruce's flying apparatus.

In ninety minutes Bruce arrived
(he'd fled unscathed) in Moscow.
None who chased could catch the man—
but here is what they followed:

a car he'd made, Aeolian,
with steel and copper gears,
with blades and clamps and springs agleam—
he'd had it for a year.

новенький и блестящий, под дождем и под градом
долго стоял Дворцовой площади он, пылясь,
по середине ровно — царским мешал парадам.
«Что за штука такая здесь собирает грязь?» —

вопрошали, — ан вот что вышло. — А всё наука, —
Брюс не в России, точно, выучился всему,
впрочем, никто не знает, подлинно ли? А ну-ка
разбери после стольких лет. Говорят, уму

Восхищение необычными способностями Брюса. — Попытка объяснить их происхождение Божественным промыслом. — Рассуждение в защиту Веры.

он и природе только собственным благодарен:
необычайным даром Бог наделил его, —
потому-то и сталось, что не мужик, не барин,
но человек обычный стал пытать естество:

переплавлять в горниле пламенном, точной мерой
измерять кропотливо, взвешивать на весах, —
по всему и выходит: сомневайся, но веруй. —
А пока что в московских кружится небесах

Брюс на своем ретивом аэроветролете,
солнце застеневая, — уже за кругом круг, —
ниже, — гудят моторы, скорый конец работе
предвкушая, — и смолкли неожиданно, вдруг.

Мягкая посадка на Сухаревской площади в Москве, месте последующего действия. — Народ приветствует Брюса.

Сухаревская площадь: башня — как на ладони
перевернутый кубок, — валом валит народ
сонные зенки пялить. Шум, суматоха, кони
бьются, храпят в испуге, — горе наоборот.

В колокола колотят. — Долго не выбирая,
башню Брюс, что скворешню облюбовал скворец.
Вот неделя проходит, пролетает вторая,
третья течет неспешно, — протекла наконец.

Выбор будущего места жительства.

It sat some time in Palace Square,
through rain, hail, parades.
"What's this whatsit do?" some folks
inquired, "take up space?"

And now they had their answer: science!
Bruce learned it all abroad.
And was it real, you're asking? Who knows!
The answer's known to God.

Admiration for Bruce's unusual capabilities. An attempt to demonstrate their source in divine providence. A treatise in defense of Faith.

Some say his genius is innate,
but God gaveth his talent.
Of standard stock—not prince or slave—
Bruce tests Nature's elements.

Man smelts inside the crucible,
he gauges what's perceived;
he makes painstaking measurements—
yes! but doubt *while* you believe.

Meanwhile Bruce's fiery mount
floats through Moscow's skies,
his Aeolian car blocks out the light—
it loops before our eyes

then circles down, its motor's hum
decresendoes to its ending—
it sails into a quietude
that always was impending.

A soft landing on Sukharev Square in Moscow, the locus of subsequent action. The people greet Bruce.

Behold Sukharev Square and Tower.
The tower's a goblet toppled
on an open palm. The common folk
walk by wide-eyed and ogle.

Cries, confusion: spooked drays rear
and neigh. Their driver glowers.
The bells soon sound. No need to choose—
Bruce settles in the tower,

Choosing a future place of residence.

Трудно составить полный список его занятий,
дел великих и малых перечень за такой
срок, — бумаги не хватит, ни замков, ни печатей,
чтобы хранить в архиве, — вреден ему покой.

Начало точного перечня разнообразных занятий Брюса.

Брюс по столам расставил пузырьки да подзоры
и распихал по полкам тыщи тяжелых книг,
карт, чертежей и планов переворочал горы, —
ногу поставить негде, но разобраться в них

Создание порядка из хаоса для начала работы.

некому, кроме Брюса. — Вот алфавит вселенной
перелагает с тарабарского языка,
брови насупя, — ради пользы, не славы бренной
для изводить чернила не устает рука

Перевод астрономического календаря.

правая: пишет, пишет непонятные знаки,
шепчет под нос по-русски звездные имена,
с небом сверяет, видит светы в кромешном мраке, —
ночи ему открыта широта, глубина.

Вот составляет карту Русских земель, дотошно
всё, что в пути приметил сверху, летя в Москву
из Петербурга, денно изображает, нощно, —
каждой речке и взгорку, всякому место рву,

Начертание полной географической карты России.

just like a starling set to nest.
A week goes by, then two,
a third is slowly eking out—
until at last we're through.

It's hard to tell what he did up there,
to delineate his deeds;
There aren't enough archives or books
to record all he achieved.

The beginning of a complete list of Bruce's diverse activities.

He sorted vials and set out loupes,
then shelved a thousand tomes.
He moved mountains of maps, designs—
there was no room in his room.

The first business of the day: creating order from chaos.

Of course no one else understood
these sheets. Bruce was unique.
He transcribed the stars' cryptic codes.
He had expert technique.

Translating heavens' alphabet,
he traces out new signs.
His tireless right hand exhausts
the inkwell with his lines.

Translating the astronomical calendar.

It's for the common good—
not senseless fame—he writes
these names of stars, these obscure runes
in the tongue of Muscovites.

He mutters newfound words, then checks
them all against the heavens;
the starry light, its bounds and depths—
nothing's hidden from him.

And now he draws a perfect map
of Petersburg to Moscow,
as seen in-flight, both day and night,
each hillock and each furrow,

Drawing a complete geographical map of Russia.

лугу и перелеску определяет, — берег,
линией непрерывной из-вива-ющий-ся,
резко проливом узким, где проплывает Беринг,
отделил от Америк, — нате, мол, наша — вся!

Вот она — на медведя всклоченного похожа:
с ревом огромной мордой вертит по сторонам,
стоя на задних лапах, дыбором мех, и кожа
на животе слоится, — не подходите к нам. —

Подробное описание земель Российских.

Точкою обозначив сердце, свернул в четыре. —
После обыкновенный на столбцы да ряды
лист разграфил, названья всех елементов в мире
в них начертал, чтоб ясно, что за чем и куды:

Составление первой периодической системы химических элементов, впоследствии утерянной.

огнь и вода, земля и воздух в особых клетках,
ибо они основа, в них от аза до ять,
от минералов частых все до кристаллов редких,
даже стекло простое скрыто — ни дать ни взять.

Дабы не было скучно одному без супруги,
не отыскав достойной пары средь смертных жен,
из цветов разновидных смастерил на досуге
девушку — как живую, — новый Пигмалион:

волосы — георгины, очи — фиалки, руки —
лилии, розы — губы, ландыши — зубы, мак —
щеки; всё остальное флоксами — по науке —
и гладиолусами тело скрепил вот так

Творение по примеру Пигмалиона тела своей невесты из разных садовых и полевых цветов. — Наречение ее латинским именем Флора. — Сожаление по поводу невозможности вложить в нее человеческую душу.

each meadow, copse, and rivulet,
even the coast laid out
in endless, winding, unbroken lines,
the water's whereabouts

through narrow straits, the Bering Sea
that bounds us from the thrust of
America, as if to say,
look here: all this is Russia!

And Russia's like a reared-up bear
with matted fur. She's hungry.
Her skin hangs loose, her muzzle turns
to roar: don't touch me!

A detailed description of the Russian lands.

Bruce marks its heart with a small dot
then folds it all away.
He draws a grid on a fresh sheet
and begins to survey

the elements of all the world
in columns and long rows.
He orders them, what follows what,
till it's clear where each thing goes:

Compilation of the first periodic table of the chemical elements, subsequently lost.

fire and water, the earth and air,
basics that hold it all,
the crystals rare, the plainest grass,
the common minerals.

He then decides he would be bored
to live without a wife,
but since no mortal maidens rank
he builds one real as life;

Creation of his bride's body, in the manner of Pygmalion, using various garden blooms and wild-flowers. She is given the Latin name Flora. Regret that a human soul cannot be instilled in her.

stringing flowers of varied hues,
our new Pygmalion
gives her dahlia hair, violet eyes,
and lips rosarium;

и нарек по науке — как положено — Флорой
Арчимбольдовной, нет лишь в ней души: посмотреть
издали — незаметно, — взрачной она и спорой
по хозяйству казалась. — Этот продолжен впредь

список длиннющий будет. — Только в одном оконце
свет по ночам златится в непроглядной Москве:
то не свеча горела там на столе, но солнце
в склянке грушеобразной, — как не пойти молве,

Ночные бдения Брюса при электрическом освещении вызывают подозрения у московских обывателей. — Состав населения града Москвы.

прямо- да кривотолкам, друг обгоняя друга. —
Темный в Москве народец проживает: купцы,
городовые, воры, прочие — их прислуга, —
хера никто не может отличить ото *рцы*.

Месяцу быть луною полною надоело:
плавно пошел на убыль и превратился в серп. —
Слухи напротив — пухнут, приобретая тело:
бают, Москве от Брюса будет один ущерб;

Распространяющиеся слухи о том, что Брюс наложил тайный запрет на мелкие и крупные преступления.

her teeth are lilies-of-the-valley,
white as that flower's cups;
she has poppies for cheeks; the rest
of her he builds from phlox.

Her flesh he binds with gladiolus,
then calls her, as custom
states, Flora Archimboldovna.
One thing alone was missing:

a soul, alas! But barring that,
nothing about her was wrong.
She's comely, prudent, clever, tidy.
(There's more to say anon.)

Bruce's evening vigils, illuminated by means of electricity, make Moscow suspicious. The composition of Moscow's population.

At night a single window glows
in all the pierceless dark
of Moscow. This little golden light
is not a candle's wick

burning late upon a table—
it's a small sun locked
in one of Bruce's pear-shaped bottles.
How could folks not talk?

How could rumors not ripple outward?
Lackwits live in Moscow—
merchants, sentries, thieves, and servants—
and none knows ass from elbow.

Rumors circulate that Bruce has enacted a secret ban on crime, both petty and heinous.

The moon now finishes her fullness.
She takes the loss in stride,
waning now, now come to crescent.
Rumors, though, spread wide

and swell, fattened by all the people
who prattle about Bruce,
certain that his presence will bring
ill-profit, even loose

будто купцам-барыгам перестала на рынке
праведная торговля приносить барыши;
жить невозможно стало более по старинке, —
делать — что хочешь делай, но грешить — не греши.

Череда происшествий на рынке, подтверждающих слухи.

Вот восседает в лавке здоровенный купчище,
думает, как обмерить или обвесить как
несмышленый народец попроворней, почище, —
глядь, из угла вылазит семисаженный рак,

Брюс трижды пресекает происки рыночных обманщиков «отводом глаз». — Животные страхи нечистых на руку купцов. — Непрекращающийся крик и шум и вопль испуганных. — Веселый смех добродушной толпы.

желтую пасть разинул, страшные тянет клешни,
кой-чего так и хочет откусить у купца, —
бедному в самом деле чудится свет нездешний, —
весь дрожит от испуга, спал румянец с лица,

ни закричать не может, и не кричать нет мочи:
крупным градом холодный катится пот со лба, —
как заголосит, словно режут его. — Короче:
мигом на зов протяжный соберется толпа, —

а ничего и нету, точно и не бывало
вовсе, — семисаженный рак исчез, как возник.
От души посмеялись: «Мало тебе, мол, мала!» —
В лавке соседней душераздирающий крик. —

Все — туда. — Вместо узких глаз у купца квадраты; —
говорит, набежала всякая свинота,
все персидские ткани на сто рублев подраты, —
огляделись — и гогот в сорок четыре рта

the coins from two-bit traders' pockets.
The market vendors raise a din.
But hear this: Man, do what you will,
be free, but just don't sin!

Take *this* massive merchant, a mountain
who looms above his wares;
he spends his days finding new ways
to short the weight or pare

A sequence of events at the market confirms the rumors.

the cut he gives the unsuspecting.
But look! A massive crab
is scuttling from a corner! It's keen
to cleave the sweetest slab

With his own "sleight of hand," Bruce thrice confounds the market vendors' shifty stratagems. The sticky-fingered stall-keepers' animal terror. Unending din, the shouts and wails of the terrorized. The good-natured crowd's carefree laughter.

of merchant. Its yellow maw, its claws
so cruel, size up the vendor—
till our poor fellow, pale with fear,
can taste his own hereafter.

He can neither move nor cry,
his sweat cascades like hail.
He's pale, too weak to shriek, until
he caterwauls and wails

like bloody murder. And then the crowds
converge around the bloke.
They find no crab; they blink their eyes.
It all went up in smoke.

Then laughing, tears astream, they hoot,
"The jest should have been crueler!"
Then a second wail, a second booth—
they all rush quickly over.

That trader's eyes now bulge to tell
of monsters in *his* tent,
of all the rubles lost when all
his Persian cloths were rent.

как раздастся: всё цело, всё — ничего и нету,
точно и не бывало вовсе, — стоят, галдят:
«Что за диво такое явлено нынче свету?» —
Вдруг — по приказу словно — все подымают взгляд,

а на балконе башни Сухаревой с усмешкой
по-над всею Москвою возвышается Брюс, —
так, склонясь над доскою шахматной, каждой пешкой
правит гроссмейстер, черно-белый тревожа ус.

Брюс забавляется происходящим.

Купчикам весь порядок глаз испортил отводом:
неулыбчивы решки, агрессивны орлы;
городовые больше не играют народом,
и воровать боятся воры, — на Брюса злы

от велика до мала — нет никакого спасу. —
«Что за жизнь наступила? — естество вопиет!» —
Бьют челом государю, жалуясь. — Внемля гласу
подданных, неотложно — разобут, разодет —

Негодование известной части населения на насмешки Брюса. — Челобитье обиженных подданных царю. — Петр срочным порядком выезжает в Москву для выяснения обстоятельств дела Брюса. — Описание царского поезда.

едет в командировку царь со своею свитой:
по бокам генералы с умным видом сидят;
тянет на сотню пушек колокол перелитый,
киверами сверкая, сотня бравых солдат.

The crowd looked on, two-score strong,
before they burst in gales
of laughter. His carpets were whole,
untouched, and spread for sale.

Nothing really had gone wrong,
and so the rabble mused:
"What's this? A wonder? A world awry?"
At that, as if on cue,

Bruce's amusement at these occurrences.

Bruce appeared above them, smirking.
The crowd craned its neck
to see the balcony atop
Sukharev Tower, the deck

that held our hero and Grand Master.
The people were his pawns,
the city his chessboard. He looms,
smooths his moustache, yawns.

Bruce's mockery makes a certain segment of the population indignant. The offended subjects kowtow to their Tsar. Peter leaves for Moscow immediately to investigate the situation with Bruce. A description of the imperial train.

The merchants' tricks were known, their luck
run out, the tables turned;
the thieves wouldn't thieve, nor sentries glare:
the lot of them all burned

with rage against this Bruce unbeaten.
"Our lives have gone to the dogs!"
the claimants tell the Tsar. He hears,
and leaves—uncloaked, unshod—

such was his haste. He gave the call:
"Away! We'll hie us thither."
His generals beside him strut,
his soldiers' visors glimmer

and number in the hundred, men
who tug their hundred cannon,
together forged from one church bell
by old Ivan Motorin.

Брюсу о том, что поезд царский еще не близко,
стало уже известно из темноты зеркал, —
занят делами мирно. — Вот продолженье списка
дел великих и малых, коими просверкал

Извещение Брюса о готовящемся нашествии неприятеля. — Продолжение точного перечня разнообразных занятий Брюса.

яркою на Российском небосклоне кометой
Брюс. — От жары в июле и духоты, увы,
нету спасенья, — солнце так и палит над этой
частью света, в которой жирный паук Москвы

сплел свою паутину. — Брюс переплавил в тигле
уголь и воду в ступе пестиком растолок,
после смешал всё вместе — брызги углов достигли,
выпарил на жаровне — взмыли под потолок

Химические опыты. — Снег, выпавший во время летнего зноя. — Радость детей. — Злоба представителей власти.

клубы седые, — вышел, — всё порошком снаружи
белым слегка посыпал — и повернул домой:
снег повалил январский, льдом затянуло лужи,
хоть на коньках катайся, — холодно, как зимой.

Вот накатались вдоволь тут на салазках дети
и в снежки наигрались, — городовые лишь
согреваются злобой: «Ничего, на рассвете
ты, мол, у нас попляшешь — живо заговоришь!» —

К вечеру снег растаял — судам да пересудам,
толкам да разговорам новый открыт простор. —
Брюс у себя закрылся, занят каким-то чудом
очередным, а старый на него из-за штор

Распространение новых и новых слухов. — Продолжение ночных бдений. — Спящая Флора.

But Bruce could soon deduce how far
the Tsar still had to journey.
His magic mirror showed but dark—
and so he worked serenely.

Bruce is informed of the enemy's impending invasion. The continuation of the complete list of Bruce's diverse activities.

Here are his deeds both great and small,
the record now is permanent.
O'er Russia's earth our Bruce shines bright,
a comet in the firmament.

There's no relief from summer's heat
when sunlight roasts that corner
of earth where Moscow's spun her web—
that city's like a spider.

So Bruce melts coal in a crucible,
grinds water to a powder,
mixes it all—this splatters his room—
and heats it in a brazier.

Chemical experiments. Snow falling in the heat of summer. The children's exultation. The ire of the authorities.

A cloud now swells, full grey and huge,
from out his boiled-down mix;
he heads outside to cast his blend
wherever it will drift.

The snow is falling when he's back,
the cold won't soon abate.
A blizzard blankets all, and ice
is thick enough to skate.

But soon the kids no longer sled,
they've had their fill of snowballs.
The sentries warm themselves with thoughts
of imminent reprisal:

"By God, we'll make you dance, dear Bruce—
you'll spill your guts easy."
By night the snow melts; its absence
fills with censure and hearsay.

Ever more rumors abound. Resumption of the evening vigils. The sleeping Flora.

пристально смотрит месяц, что пятак на червонце:
дремлют, на полках стоя, тыщи тяжелых книг,
в грушеобразной склянке светит, сверкая, солнце,
девушки сон цветочной безмятежен и тих, —

жаль, что души в ней нету. — Бога с жаром и силой
Брюс о России просит, молится за Москву:
«Господи, если можешь, сохрани и помилуй!» —
Вдруг окликает кто-то — как во сне — наяву, —

Молитвы и просьбы Брюса о благоденствии сей страны. — Явление незримого ангела-хранителя. — Избранничество Брюса. — Приглашение к путешествию.

голос такой знакомый и незнакомый разом:
«Человече! угодны Богу твой твердый нрав,
дух твой неугомонный, твой дерзновенный разум, —
ты правотой небесной, как и земною, прав.

Явлено и открыто было тебе немало
на земле и на небе, — зримого мира весь
ясен состав согласный от конца до начала,
о заочном же — верных недостаточно здесь

сведений по причине односторонней связи:
как бы туда хотелось хоть на миг заглянуть
многим, но тщетно; ты же — избран — не в пересказе
знать — воочию видеть и удивляться». — Путь:

But Bruce has locked his shutters tight,
concocting his next feat;
the moon's a penny peering in
that envies a gold piece.

His sun still fills its pear-shaped bottle,
each tome sleeps on its shelf;
his flower-girl can sleep so calm—
a shame she's soulless herself.

Meanwhile Bruce appeals to God
to give Moscow his mercy;
he hotly cries, "Lord, will you grant
your pardon and your safety?"

Bruce's entreaties and prayers for the country's prosperity. An invisible guardian angel appears. Bruce is chosen. An invitation to a journey.

Suddenly someone responds—
dream-like, but this is true—
a voice like one that Bruce has known
but foreign, somehow, too:

"O Man! Your steady disposition,
quick spirit, and daring mind
are pleasing to God who deems you just,
a righteous son of mankind.

Much on earth is known to you,
and heaven's likewise revealed;
the harmony of the visible world
is clear from head to heel.

But man can scarcely scrounge a truth
from out the world *un*seen—
the masses yearn to glimpse those forms,
but they all look in vain.

You're chosen, though, to know firsthand,
to see and be amazed;
what follows, Bruce, defies all words."
Behold, this is the way:

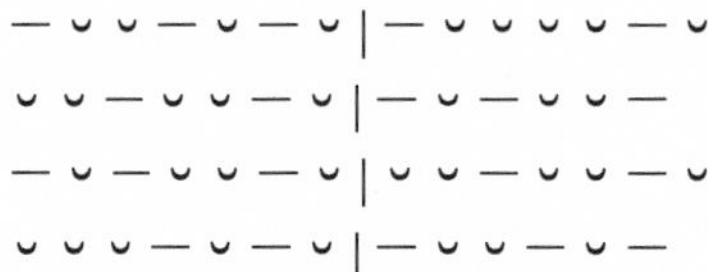

Не описать полета духа языком плоти:
Брюсу открылась бездна, пламенных звезд полна, —
хор и орган, гласящий Господа в каждой ноте;
блещет своей обратной стороною луна;

точкою синеватой стала земля, златистой —
солнце, созвездий грозды, что в траве светляки,
точно толпа цыганок, прозвеневших монистой,
словно огни деревни рядом — и — далеки,

так миры промелькнули. — Светом из ниоткуда
озарено пространство, — от незримых светил
нет ни жара, ни хлада. — Необъятное чудо,
где ни тел и ни теней, кто хоть раз посетил,

счастлив! — «Слова земные беспомощны и скудны
славу сокровищ горних изобразить, пока
оглушительно-ярок день не наступит Судный,
возвещая рожденье нового языка —

Оставление Брюсова тела его же духом. — Точное изображение невидимого полета в надмирные выси. —Развернутое описание всего, что мелькнуло перед внутренним взором во время быстрого перелета сквозь вселенную. — Достижение цели.

Явленные Брюсу наднебесные таинства. — Пророчества о мире.

Bruce's soul leaves his body. A precise description of his unseen flight into the empyrean realm. A meticulous description of all that flashed before his internal gaze during his rapid flight through the universe. Arrival at the destination.

˘ / ˘ / ˘ / ˘ /
/ ˘ ˘ / ˘ /
˘ / ˘ / ˘ / ˘ /
˘ / ˘ / ˘ ˘ /

˘ / ˘ / ˘ ˘ / ˘ /
˘ / ˘ / ˘ / ˘
˘ / ˘ / ˘ / ˘ /
˘ / ˘ / ˘ / ˘

The soul in flight can't be described
in meager, earthly words.
Bruce saw a vast abyss replete
with fiery stars and chords,

with choirs and organs praising God,
the moon's dark side aglow,
the earth receded to a dot,
the sun a golden mote.

The clustered constellations pass
like fireflies in meadows,
like necklaced coins 'round gypsy girls,
or distant towns aglow.

So too did all the worlds flash by.
Then light illumed that maw
of black, from lamp not hot or cold
or seen, but full of awe

we cannot fathom. Bodies, shadows—
they've no place in this abyss.
Yet he who's glimpsed it once could live
in utmost happiness!

Sublime mysteries are revealed to Bruce. A prophecy regarding the end of the world.

"Earthly words are helpless, paltry,
to show the true renown
of treasures from the Mount—but when
the Day of Judgment dawns,

сплава глаголов грозных и тяжелых наречий;
на равновесных чашах вспыхнут добро и зло;
обернется разлука неожиданной встречей, —
слово было в начале, будет в конце число». —

Вестником расторопным, неустанным вожатым
Брюса такой знакомый и незнакомый глас
верно сопровождает по небесам тройчатым,
объясняя, толкуя зримое и от глаз

Брюс в сопровождении ангела-хранителя посещает три неба: Отца, Сына и Святого Духа.

скрытое пеленою: «Нынче, прежде и после
связаны воедино, тесно сопряжены, —
разница небольшая меж временами осле-
пления и прозрений, громов и тишины.

Всех времен и событий вот амбарная книга, —
в ней по порядку войны, бедствия, мятежи
перечислены, — роспись до последнего мига». —
Брюс вопрошает: «Что же будет со мной, скажи?» —

Книга судеб. — Пророчества о будущем. — Дарование Брюсу временного бессмертия для девяти земных жизней. — Принятие других даров: жидкого, твердого и газообразного. — Напоминание о бренности всего мирского и об ограниченности человеческих возможностей в сравнении с Божественной волей.

«Душ обитель прозрачных посетив и покинув,
как изо сна восхищен, так и вернешься в сон,
наделенный дарами щедро, — ни райских кринов,
ни сковородок адских — ты на земле нужон,

deafening, dazzling, it will bring
a language newly born
from alloy forged of fearsome verbs
and adverbs great and stern;

Good and evil will level the scale
with weights of equal measure.
In the beginning was the Word;
the end will be a Number."

This voice at once both known and not,
this guide and skillful herald,
leads Bruce through heaven's triple tiers
describing both what's veiled

Bruce, attended by his guardian angel, sojourns in the three heavens of the Father, the Son, and the Holy Spirit.

and visible, expounding all
flawlessly for our hero:
"The present and the past are linked—
they're one with all that follows.

Compare the moment you go blind
with when you regain sight:
the difference is the time between
a thunderclap and quiet.

And here's the reckoning book that holds
all time and all events.
It inventories wars, revolts,
and plagues to the last second."

The book of fate. A prophecy about the future. Bruce is granted provisional immortality, for the span of nine earthly lives. Other gifts are bestowed: liquid, solid, and gas. A reminder of the frailty of earthly things and of the poverty of Man's capabilities in comparison to God's will.

Bruce asks, "What is to be my fate?"
The voice gives this reply:
"This home of souls intangible
you've seen, and now pass by,

will soon give way to sleep just as
from sleep you once were taken,
but you'll return with ample gifts:
you're the one God's chosen.

ибо избранник Божий. — Смерти кривых иголок
больше не бойся, — девять тел износишь до дыр. —
На три дара небесных: склянку с росою, сколок
тверди да мех надутый, где заключен эфир

животворящий. — Помни: всё, что здесь без изъяна,
в небесах неподвижных, то на земле, увы,
переменно и тленно; человек — обезьяна
Божья — не прыгнет выше собственной головы». —

Путь обратный подобен вычерченному выше:
снова мелькнули звезды — солнце — луна — земля;
царский в дороге поезд — вот московские крыши —
вот купола соборов — славный оплот кремля;

Возвращение на землю, столь же стремительное, как и взлет. — Утро.

Сухаревская площадь: башня — как на ладони
перевернутый кубок, — мещет рассвет лучи,
медленно подымая в золоченой короне
голову, — блекнет пламя негасимой свечи.

Бодрствующий со спящим соединился телом
дух, — и, вздрогнув, проснулся Брюс от толчка, в себя
приходя постепенно: сон цветной черно-белым
показался, мгновенным — длительное, рябя

Брюс очнулся как ни в чем не бывало. — Различия между сном и явью значительны. — Небесные дары становятся неприметными земными вещами.

Skillets in hell or lilies in heaven,
you need not dwell on either.
The earth now calls. You needn't fear
Death's crooked needles,

for you can wear out earthly bodies—
nine of them, or more.
Now take the following gifts divine:
a phial of dew, a sliver

of heaven, and this skin that fills
to hold life-giving ether.
Remember though: whatever's flawless
here in heaven ceaseless

will be—alas!—quite changeable
on earth. To wit: it withers.
Man's a monkey to God; he cannot
grasp more than he reaches."

The path back home is like the one
above: the sun and stars,
the moon and earth flash past, a train
en route that bears the Tsar,

Bruce alights back on Earth as swiftly as he left it. Morning.

the Moscow rooftops. See the churches,
the Kremlin's parapets
and bulwarks; there's Sukharev Square,
its tower like a goblet

upturned upon an open palm.
The sunrise lifts its single
crown, sending gold rays sweeping.
The ever-burning candle's

snuffed inside its pear-shaped bottle.
See: Bruce's waking soul
rejoins his sleeping body. He bolts
upright, wakes with a jolt—

Bruce awakens as though nothing had happened. The significant differences between dream and reality. The heavenly gifts become plain, earthly things.

в затуманенном взоре взветренными вихрами.
Но три дара небесных целы: не прорван мех,
не расколота склянка, краегранник, во храме
освященный заочном, невредимее всех, —

блещет, искря. — Склонился первым делом ко Флоре,
вдунул эфир со свистом Брюс погруженной в сон —
сердце в груди забилось, вспыхнула страсть во взоре,
и — любовью взаимной ей отвечает он:

Один из даров Брюс использует для водушевления Флоры. — Любовь.

. . . .
. . . .
. . . .
. . . .

А тем временем царский поезд въезжает в город:
разноцветные флаги плещутся на ветру;
черных, седых и рыжих толпы усов и бород, —
с хлебом-солью выходит Брюс навстречу Петру.

Петр именным указом пообещал награды
тем, кто поймает Брюса, — зверь бежит на ловца! —
«Не силком, — несказанно городовые рады, —
наконец-то попалась волку в лапы овца!» —

Торжественный въезд Петра в Москву. — Происходящие при этом невероятные события. — Троекратный выход мнимых Брюсов во сретенье Петру. — Язва. — Гнев.

and so his lengthy, rainbow'd dream
recedes into gray tones.
It flashes past his baffled gaze
like whirlwinds whipped and blown.

At least his three heavenly gifts
remained in his possession:
the skin still taut, the phial still whole,
the fragment of empyrean—

faceted, flashing—so blessed
in that timeless cathedral.
On earth they can't be broken, so Bruce—
seeing something useful—

now blows the ether into his wife
(Good Flora's deep in slumber.)
Her heart now beats; her eyes flash love.
This love is Bruce's answer:

Bruce uses one of the gifts to animate Flora. Love.

....
....
....
....

Meanwhile the train of the Tsar arrives,
its colored flags aflapping;
the beards come too, in many hues—
black and red moustaches.

Peter's ceremonial entry into Moscow. The astonishing events attending it. Illusory Bruces come out three times to meet Peter. A scourge. Wrath.

But look! There's Bruce! He's bringing salt
and bread right out to Peter!
And this after the Tsar's decree:
a reward to Bruce's captor!

It seems the prey to hunter flees.
The sentries are rejoicing:
"We haven't moved a muscle yet,
but this sheep we'll soon be wolfing!"

Навалились, скрутили, потащили в участок. —
С хлебом-солью выходит Брюс навстречу царю
как ни в чем не бывало. — Снова скрутили: «Нас так
не провести!» — «Покорно, — он им, — благодарю!» —

Только не тут-то было: вязан и шит не лыком,
с хлебом-солью выходит снова Брюс из толпы. —
Гнев, о богиня, грозный вспыхнул в Петре Великом, —
рвет и мечет: «Ужели все, как один, глупы? —

Идиоты! Тупицы! Хоть бы вы поредели!
Чтоб вас...» — Не доверяя бородам и усам,
сам разобраться хочет в этом опасном деле,
допросить по порядку Брюса каждого сам. —

Петр лично учиняет мнимым Брюсам допрос с пристрастием.

Выяснилось: все трое как две капли похожи, —
царь со слововоротом: «Ай, иду, судия!» —
точно Нептун, ярится, вержа трезубцем: «Кто же
Брюс из вас настоящий, из троих?» — «Я!» — «Я!» — «Я!» —

«Что за дикое слово? — Срочно из алфавита
вычеркнуть эту букву, из словаря — долой!» —
Расстрелять предлагает поодиночке свита
царская, — Петр допетрил: «Всех отпустить домой!» —

Ничего не добившись, царь разгневан еще больше. — Почувствовав какой-то подвох, он приказывает отпустить их на все четыре стороны.

They fall on him and wrench him down;
they drag him to the station.
But look! There's Bruce, with bread and salt,
as if nothing had happened.

And so they wrench him down once more:
"We won't fall for your tricks!"
"I thank you humbly," he replies,
but knows he isn't licked.

Again our Bruce brings bread and salt,
the third to leave the crowd.
O Goddess Ancient, O Fury Horrid,
you've sparked the Tsar to shout

and froth: "Are they witless to a man?
Those idiotic sentries!
Rot in hell! I'll soon find better
men than them, and plenty."

Peter personally conducts a physical interrogation of the illusory Bruces.

Peter the Great has lost all faith
in his moustaches and beards;
this treachery, he thinks, deserves
his own attention. He hears

and queries the Bruces one by one.
They're like three peas in a pod.
"Dammit, I'm mad!" the Tsar cries out,
their exasperated god.

He strides toward them, spiteful Neptune,
his trident poised to fly—
"Which Bruce in three's the real one?"
"I!" "I!" "I!"

"Is that some kind of curse word now?"
his petty generals whine.
"Let's cut it from the alphabet!
The dictionary's fine

Unable to beat anything out of the Bruces, the Tsar is further incensed. He senses a deception and commands them to make themselves scarce.

предварительно Брюса каждого припечатав
в зубы своим огромным царственным кулаком,
будто бы на дежурстве задремавших солдатов
перед Преображенским лейб-гвардейским полком.

Только глядь: никакие это не Брюсы — тройка
генералов суровых битая предстоит, —
трут распухшие скулы, но на вопросы бойко
отвечают, а зуб-то затаен ядовит:

Брюсы оказываются простыми царскими генералами.

«Доберемся до Брюса, — не покажется мало! —
чтоб ему пусто было! — будет он наших знать!» —
троица чуть со злости трости не изломала. —
Петр командует: «Брюса мне подать!» — «Ать-два, ать!» —

Озлобленные генералы по приказу Петра выступают в поход против Брюса.

раздается да цокот с топотом вперемежку
вдоль по Третьему Риму, пробуждая от сна. —
Окна блестят навстречу, открываясь. Насмешку
прячет в ладони всякий, свесившись из окна.

Брюс преспокойно в башне наслаждается Флорой;
медленно попивает кофе, какао, чай;
в ноздри табак влагает. — С площади, на которой
яблоку выпасть негде, слышно: «Гостей встречай-

Ожидающий незваных гостей Брюс невозмутимо предается осмысленному отдыху. — Генералы тщетно пытаются выманить его из башни.

without it!" They suggest shooting
this pesky, Bruce-ish trio
but Peter the Great thinks better:
"Let all three Bruces go."

But first he'll smash three sets of teeth
with his imperial fist,
as if he'd caught three soldiers sleeping
while standing at their post.

But look! The Bruces aren't Bruces now,
they're generals, disheveled.
They stand there stern and rub their jaws,
quite thoroughly bedeviled.

The Bruces turn out to be nothing more than the Tsar's generals.

"Bruce'll be sorry once he's caught!"
they say, nursing new grudges.
Though puzzled by these tricks, they swear,
"He'll soon be in our clutches!"

At Peter's command, the enraged generals march out against Bruce.

They spew abuse and damn dear Bruce.
They break their small batons.
But Peter growls, "Bring him to me!"
then "Forward troops! March on!"

A clatter of hooves, the drummer's boom—
they wake up all Third Rome.
The windows light, folks hide their smirks,
and gawk from in their homes.

But Bruce enjoys his Flora's love
atop his tower tranquil.
They've coffee, cocoa, tea, and snuff,
the latter so delightful.

The unfazed Bruce, awaiting his uninvited guests, takes his ease in sensible diversions. The generals vainly strive to entice him from his tower.

The Square below is packed with viewers,
they're crowded like sardines.
"Welcome your guests!" they shout to Bruce.
There is a new decree:

те! — По указу орден Брюсу на красной ленте
жалует царь и, чтобы не сидеть на бобах,
премию. — Выходите, получите, наденьте,
а не то, мол, из пушек враз по башне бабах».

Ядра набиты туго, пылкий засыпан порох
в узкие жерла, — только спичкой голландской чирк,
как шарахнет, — подспорье в неразрешимых спорах.
Брюс — не Брюс, если эта екзекуция в цирк

не превратится. — Долго думать ему не надо,
как напасть посмешнее от себя отвести, —
пушки послушны Брюсу. — Грянула канонада, —
в небо взлетело разноцветное конфетти,

яблоки золотые, пряники да конфеты, —
оседают неспешно прямо в руки. — «Ура!» —
Отступила, хлопушки водрузив на лафеты,
артирелия. — Вскоре перед очи Петра

с жалобами на Брюса генералы предстали:
«Осрамил! Опозорил!» — Царь верхом на коне:
«Сам, — говорит, — поеду», — точно на пьедестале
громокаменном тусклый памятник Фальконе

Умело подготовленную осаду Сухаревой башни Брюс превращает в очередную потеху. — Фейерверк. — Царские генералы несолоно хлебавши возвращаются к Петру, негодуя на обидчика. — Государь сам пытается предпринять решительный штурм.

the Tsar has granted Bruce a medal
with ribbon red and gold.
"Take your money, stock your pantry!
The prize befits the bold.

Your other option ain't so pretty:
this cannon blasts your belfry."
Indeed its powder had been tamped,
its shot was sitting snugly,

the narrow barrel simply needed
the skritch of a sulphur match…
then *boom!* This blast would prove a boon
in any lengthy clash.

But true to form our Bruce has found
a way to make this conflict
comic. He's quick to glean the means
of halting pyrotechnics.

Bruce turns the well-laid siege of the Sukharev Tower into yet another amusement. Fireworks. The Tsar's generals return to Peter empty-handed, railing against the offender. The sovereign attempts a full frontal assault himself.

He recommands the cannons and blasts
a thunderous cannonade;
the sky explodes with bright confetti
in great, shredded sprays,

with cookies spiced and apples golden,
the chocolates fall like rain!
The bounty lands in hands outstretched.
The Tower still remains.

The crowd is thrilled, the soldiers not.
The former cheers, "Hooray!"
while cannoneers collect pop-guns;
they're calling it a day.

The generals assemble then
to lodge complaints with Peter:
"He mocked us all! We live in shame!"
The Tsar, ahorse, just mutters:

с надписью: *Petro Primo — Catharina Secu...da,* —
n отвалилось наземь, — видно, задел ногой. —
«Но!» — и вот перед башней Сухаревой откуда
ни возьмись появился царь через миг-другой:

Упреки и угрозы Петра непокорному Брюсу. — Добрый совет последнего первому.

«Ты почто презираешь государеву служу,
Брюс, наград не приемлешь и плюешь на закон
сверху вниз? — Выходи-ка, нарушитель, наружу!
коль не хочешь остаться без дверей, без окон, —

на тебя поступило предостаточно жалоб». —
«Царь, — с балкона бросает Брюс, — хоть ты и велик,
а змеи-то не видишь, — раздавить не мешало б,
раздвоенное вырвав жало, вставить язык.

Приглашение к прощальному ужину. — Второй дар Брюс передает Петру.

Гостем будь!» — Всё готово для почестного пира. —
Флора напитки, яства подает. — «Будь здоров!» —
Между Петром и Брюсом нет ни войны, ни мира,
но ко второму ближе. — Из небесных даров

"I'll go myself." And now he looms
like Falconet's grim statue,
the one inscribed: *Petro Primo –*
Catharina Secu[ ]da.

(His foot knocked the *n* right off
the Thunderstone's inscription.)
"Now then!" he says and soon appears
at Sukharev Tower's bastion.

"Why scorn to serve your lord, dear Bruce?
You spurn being rewarded?
And why do you spit on laws from on high?
These too you've disregarded!

Bruce remains uncowed by Peter's threats and accusations. The former's sound advice to the latter.

Come out of there to open air
or I'll have to open fire.
I've heard complaints enough to blast
your precious home and spire."

"My Tsar!" Bruce calls, "you're great, no doubt,
but here you've missed the viper!
Rip out its stinger, add a tongue.
Now *that's* the way to conquer."

To which Bruce adds: "Come, join my table!"
He's gallant, keen to host.
Dear Flora offers meat and mead.
They sit, they feast, they toast!

An invitation to a farewell supper. Bruce bestows the second gift on Peter.

"God grant you health!" they each propose.
And thus what reigns 'twixt Peter
and Bruce is neither peace nor war,
though closer to the former.

In parting Bruce presents a gift—
the shard of sky, that jewel—
to Peter. Let him keep this so Rus'
renews: not mild, nor cruel,

краеугольный камень, дабы Россия крепла,
придавая значенье внешности и нутру,
в золото и порфиру наряжалась, из пепла
восставала, — прощаясь, Брюс подарил Петру.

Встал, — незаметно вышел, — в аэроветролете,
склянку с рассолом горним пред собой положив,
вместе с прекрасной Флорой прочь упорхал. — Не ждете? —
Ждите, — и Брюс вернется, — он и поныне жив!

Уход. — Третий дар Брюс оставляет себе, как залог временного бессмертия. — Надежда на возвращение Брюса.

Мой любезный читатель! заново поскорее
непринужденным взглядом эту повесть окинь;
ведай Творца и помни: дактили да хореи
не напрасно взаимозаменялись. — Аминь.

Наставление благосклонному читателю сей повести. — Конец.

1995—1999

but wise enough to prize in Man
his essence, not his fashions.
May gold and porphyry adorn
this land reborn from ashes.

Bruce stands, slips out, and stows the phial
of hallowed brine inside
his magic aero. He boards with Flora.
They lift and climb the skies.

Departure. Bruce keeps the third gift for himself, as a pledge against his provisional immortality. Hope for Bruce's return.

And you: why don't you wait awhile?
Take off your coat, and stay.
In time your Bruce *will* reappear.
He's still alive today!

Dear Reader: cast your carefree gaze
once more upon this story.
Don't tarry. Know the Lord is God,
and His is all the glory.

Exhortation to the gracious reader of this tale. Finish.

Remember too this ballad meter
that issued from my pen;
these iambs, rhymes, and substitutions
were not in vain. Amen.

1995 – 1999

III.

Исповедь переписчика

Я — переписчик, обитель святую лет
не покидавший тридцать иль сорок,
знаю немного: книга мертва, если нет
в ней ни описок, ни оговорок;
суть на полях расположена и меж строк,
в буквицах явлена, в титлах скрыта;
время нещадно написанного песок
хрупкий сквозь крупное сеет сито.

Я — переписчик, одежда моя проста,
златом не блещет и перламутром
утварь, полати — для сна, для молитв — уста —,
ночь скоротать — и за дело утром:
в книге любой до конца от начала есть
то ощущение смертной битвы,
зря не одну изведешь без коего десть,
и не помогут тебе молитвы.

Я — переписчик, смиренное ремесло
дарит возможность продлиться в мире:
медленно книги ветшают, — своих число
помню до точности: три Псалтири,
двадцать Апостолов, девять Палей, семь Пчел,
пять Шестодневов, и каждый штучен, —
всё бы я мной переписанное прочел,
если бы грамоте был обучен.

2015

The Scribe's Confession

I am a scribe. I haven't left my cloister
  in lo some thirty or forty years,
but this much I know: a book's dead if no
  errata or proviso appears,
for its essence begins where the text ends,
  clear in its illumination, obscured in its title.
Time sieves the sand of what's written
  through the wire mesh of a riddle.

I am a scribe. My clothing is simple;
  my instruments don't dazzle with gold
or mother-of-pearl. I've a plank-bed to sleep on,
  lips for praying; I work while morning unfolds.
In any book you'll find a battle
  waged—from first line to *finis*—to the death,
without which no quire's completed.
  And prayers? Oh no, save your breath.

I am a scribe. My humble craft
  is my short life's lasting balm.
Books decay slowly. I remember precisely
  how many I've done: three Psalms,
twenty Apostols, and nine Palaea Historicas,
  five Hexamerons, and seven Bees.
I'd pore through all I've copied out, imbibe
  the wisdom in words, if only I could read.

2015

На приобретение тома сочинений и переводов В. И. Майкова

В. Ш.

Сто тридцать лет, Василий Ваныч
Майкóв! оставив на потом,
твоих творений толстый том
никто не читывал: ни на ночь,
огарок тепля, ни с утра,
не выспавшись восстав с одра.

Никто. — *Своя у книги каждой* —
болтали римляне — *судьба*, —
ни властелина, ни раба,
томимого духовной жаждой,
рука не трогала страниц
сих, будто кто над ухом «*цыц*».

Том неразрезанный, бескожий,
презревши переплета ков,
владельца выбирал. (Майков!
а помнишь, у тебя в прихожей
подслушивал Державин од
перерывающийся ход:

«Багряну ризу распустила
по небу тихая заря
и тем прекрасных дней царя
приход вселенной возвестила.
Прохладой полный утра час
взывает дух мой на Парнасс;

уже я лиру восприемлю,
хочу воспеть, на ней глася,
приятну песнь произнося,
что паки мир грядет на землю».

On the Acquisition of a Volume of V. I. Maikov's Works and Translations

for V. Sh.

A century and thirty, Vasily Ivanych
Maikov?! That's procrastination.
Your creations stretch a volume
no one's ever opened. Not by the lit wick
near a bedside, nor in the AM, swept
drowsy from their four-poster, rest-

less. No one. *Every book* (or
so the Romans nattered) *has its fate*;
but neither slave or owner, weighed
low by their soul's thirst, ran fingers
through these pages, as if a stealthy
someone sealed each eye with a *shhh!*

This uncut textblock, still skin-free,
disdains the bookcloth's shackles
and thus selects its owner. (Maikov! Recall
for us Derzhavin. How he eaves-
dropped from your entranceway, heard
the halting progress of your odes:

Quiescent dawn unfurls her scarlet
robes skyward. This trumpets—to the universe—
the tsar's arrival, tsar of beauteous
days. Sweet dawn now calls my spirit
to Parnassus on its cooling breeze.
Already I've accepted the lyre, raised

music till I'm bursting. I sing
my song through her, pronounce
a melody still sweeter: that once
more peace will reach earth. It's coming.

Ну и т. д.) — Отрадна честь
его разрезать и прочесть.

Блажен избранник, но блаженней
избравший правильно стократ! —
Любимец мудрости, Сократ
новейший тыщу возражений
на это сыщет, — так и ты,
лелея детские мечты.

1998

And so forth, and so on, indeed.
I'm grateful for this cutting and reading.

So blessed is the chosen, but more
blessed by a hundred-fold is
he who's choosing. But Socrates's
offspring, wisdom's lover, will forge
for this a thousand objections—and so, it seems,
will you, cherishing childish dreams.

1998

* * *

Заря зарделась на востоке,
деревенская девка, ведущая
на привязи день
белоголовым теленком,
еще не ведающим уже
в сумороках готовящегося вечерних
ему заклания. —

Что неизбежно, то свершится. —
Одиссей хитромудрый сопутников
ослушных своих,
жаждой томимых и гладом
на диком острове, где паслось
средь пестреющих выгонов солнцево стадо,
столь постоянное

по численности, что единой
головой прирастало для убыли
в четыре зимы,
как ни старался лишенных
рассудка словом остановить,
но со слухом у чревонеистовства плохо
и нет зазрения. —

Короче, сообща напали,
кровеносную жилу надрезали
на вые быка,
дабы насытиться мясом
парным, не жаренным на костре,
и напиться рудой, — до костей был обглодан
день возвращения. —

За то погибель им досталась
всем в удел, по отдельности каждому. —

*   *   *

Dawn's rosy advent reddened the east.
Modest as a village maiden, she leads Day
like a white-faced calf
behind her, so gently tethered;
it hasn't the slightest suspicion
of the sacrifice impending, of preparations
for the evening slaughter.

What's certain will certainly happen.
Wise Ulysses, though cunning, couldn't check
his unruly troops,
tortured by their hunger, by thirst;
their savage island had pastures so
verdant and varied they'd fattened the sun-god's whole herd,
a year's worth of cattle

so perfectly constant in number
that every fourth winter it added a head,
inevitably
offered on the altar; hard as
Ulysses tried to stop them, words failed.
A flaccid belly glutting its hunger feels no pangs
of conscience, hears no sounds.

And so they attacked it together,
cut a bloody line along a vein pulsing
down a bull's strong neck,
then ate their fill of smoking meat,
fresh-killed, not roasted in a cook fire.
They gnawed the flesh off their own return, they snapped its bone,
they sucked out the marrow.

This would render death their lot, meted
out to each in turn and visited on all.

Из них не узрел
дома по странствиях многих
никто. — Единственный Одиссей,
отвлекаемый выспренним гласом от зова
утробы трубного,

не вскорости, но воротился
восвояси. — Зачем пересказывать
известное всем? —
Памороки обреченным
отшибло напрочь, — время пришло
вновь напомнить, что всё и даруется Богом,
и отнимается.

2005—2006

Not a single man
would see his home again. It was
the singular Ulysses who'd heed
that celestial voice and not the clarion call
of his grumbling belly,

thus securing a deferred (if sure)
return to hearth and homeland. But why rehearse
this same old story?
*The doomed are utterly bereft
of memory.* It's time to remind
you all again: the Lord is the source of all we have
but he can call it back.

2005 – 2006

* * *

Ты в землю врастаешь, — я мимо иду,
веселую песенку на ходу
    себе под нос напевая
про то, как — теряя златые листы —
мне кажешься неотразимою ты,
    ни мертвая, ни живая.

Ты помощи просишь, страдания дочь, —
мне нечем тебе, бедняжка, помочь:
    твои предсмертные муки
искусству возвышенному сродни,
хоть невпечатлимы ни в красках они,
    ни в камне, ни в слове, ни в звуке.

Сойдешь на нет, истаешь вот-вот, —
благой не приносящие плод
    пускай не расклеятся почки,
поскольку ты — смоковница та,
которую проклял еще до Христа
    Овидий в раздвоенной строчке.

1998

* * *

You take root in earth; I trot blithely by,
humming some happy tune
    (all by my lonesome) about how,
as your gold leaves fall, you grow
more irresistible, though you're neither
    dead nor living.

You seek help, little misery's daughter,
but what help, poor dear, might I provide?
    The death pangs attending
your final hour are just like high art, though
they refuse to be captured in sculpture,
    speech, pigment, or song.

You dwindle down to nothing,
while those buds, which bring no good
    to fruition, sit fallow—
Are you the fig our Savior damned,
or the walnut that, well before Christ's birth,
    Ovid cursed in a split verse?

1998

* * *

Мне хотелось бы собственный дом иметь
на побережье мертвом живого моря,
где над волнами небесная стонет медь,
ибо Нот и Борей, меж собою споря,
задевают воздушные колокола,
где то жар, то хлад, никогда — тепла.

Слабым зеницам закат золотой полезней,
розовый, бирюзовый, и Млечный путь,
предостерегающий от болезней,
разум смиряя, чуткий же мой ничуть
не ужаснется рокотом слух созвучий
бездны, многоглаголивой и певучей.

Сыздетства каждый отзыв ее знаком
мне, носителю редкому двух наречий,
горним, слегка коверкая, языком
то, что немощен выразить человечий,
нараспев говорящему, слов состав
вывернув наизнанку и распластав.

Что же мне остается? — невнятна долу
трудная речь и мой в пустоту звучал
глас, искажаясь, — полуспасаться, полу-
жить, обитателям смежных служа начал,
птице текучей или летучей рыбе,
в собственном доме у времени на отшибе.

1999

*　　*　　*

I wish I owned my own home
on the dead sands of a living sea,
where Notus and Boreas squabble and wrestle,
bumping the air's bells till the brassy sky
chimes high above the wave's moan—
where I shiver or fever but never feel warm.

My palsied pupils bask in the sun's gold
(its roses, its turquoise); the Milky Way
shields me from disease. All my mental tremors
are calmed. Meanwhile I'm not dismayed—
despite my soft eardrums—by the sea's garrulous
music, this polyphonous, singing abyss.

I find each sound or susurrus familiar,
for I'm that rare native-speaker of two dialects;
I've yanked base words by their root, turned them
inside out, then spread them flat
and spoken—with small alterations—what makes
human speech balk. I know vertiginous talk.

But what's left for me now that difficult speech
is inaudible in the vale? Now that I twist and prattle
in the wilderness? Might I sometimes live,
might I save myself, serving both sides
of that audience—the flying fish, the swimming flock—
in my own home, beyond time's boondocks.

1999

*   *   *

Долго ты пролежала в земле, праздная,
бесполезная, и наконец пробил
час, — очнулась от сна, подняла голову
тяжкую, распрямила хребет косный,

затрещали, хрустя, позвонки — молнии
разновидные, смертному гром страшный
грянул, гордые вдруг небеса дрогнули,
крупный град рассыпая камней облых,

превращающихся на лету в острые
вытянутые капли, сродни зернам,
жаждущим прорасти всё равно, чем бы ни
прорастать: изумрудной травой или

карим лесом, еще ли какой порослью
частой. — Ты пролежала в земле долго,
праздная, бесполезная, но — вот оно,
честно коего ты дождалась, время, —

ибо лучше проспать, суетой брезгуя,
беспробудно, недвижно свой век краткий,
чем шагами во тьме заблуждать мелкими
по ребристой поверхности на ощупь,

изредка спотыкаться, смеясь весело,
проповедуя: «Всё хорошо, славно!» —
потому-то тебя и зовут, имени
подлинного не зная, рекой — речью.

1999

* * *

Long now you've lounged in earth—futile,
useless—but at last your hour's struck;
you stirred from sleep, roused
your head's dead yoke, and aligned a crooked

spine, its vertebrae cracking like lightning—
a vast array of thunder's fearsome
peals, which lead now to the hail stones
these high heavens shed and shudder,

each transforms and tapers on the fly
into droplets thirsting to germinate, akin
to seeds, heedless of how
they'll sprout, whether as emerald herb,

hazel woods, or some other verdant
shoot… You've lounged in earth so long now—
futile, useless—but here it is, the moment
you faithfully tarried till:

for it is better to oversleep
your own short age, disdaining all
earthly vanity, than to grope dimly down
its crenellated top, stumbling across

with hesitant steps and carefree
laughter, preaching "All's well! Superb!"
That's why those who don't know
your true name call you a river of words.

1999

*   *   *

Где лопух и крапива
вдоль тропинки, сводящей в овраг,
прозябают красиво, —
на растительных нежась коврах,
звонконогий кузнечик
доживает последние дни.

Лета красного вестник,
сколотивший не Бог весть какой
капиталец на песнях,
на заслуженный выйдя покой,
предается обжорству
и медвяную хлещет росу.

Грех — невинный, бесспорно,
проводив загостившихся птиц,
в дни осеннего порно-
фестиваля рябины стриптиз
скромницы да расстриги-
бузины созерцать — не велик.

Лишь бы жизни хватило
досмотреть до конца, до звонка, —
блекнущее светило
для тебя не померкло пока,
мой кузнечик, мой ангел
поднебесный, мой Анакреон.

Мой Державин, Бетховен
на краю немоты, темноты,
ты безгрешен, — греховен
кто угодно, но только не ты,
и мытариться в райских
коридорах не долго тебе.

* * *

Where burdock and nettles,
strewn along a gulley-bound footpath,
vegetate picturesquely,
cuddling on a carpet of greens—
a thigh-chiming grasshopper
lives out his last days.

Red summer's harbinger,
whose songlets chisel a pittance
(God knows it's no
fortune!) as an earned rest nears,
he indulges in gluttony
and swigs the honeydew.

As sinners go, he's innocent—
having seen the migrated flock
home, he'll behold fall's porn-
festival, the rowan tree's modest
striptease, an elder-tree is
a monk defrocked—it's no biggie.

But if only this life
could suffice to watch it until
the end, the bell's tolling—
a sun beam that' still lingering
for you, my grasshopper, my angel
under heaven, my Anacreon.

O my Derzhavin, my Beethoven
on the brink of muteness, darkness—
you're sin-free. The sinful
mill around you, whom you're not
among. You won't languish
like a claimant in heaven's hallway.

Потому как охрана
неподкупная упреждена, —
с распростертыми рано
или поздно, но встретят. Весна
воскресения близко:
зимовать не накладно в раю!

Представляю, как зелен
ты на землю соскочишь, — вокруг
луг цветущий расстелен,
и всё тот же в овраге лопух,
и всё та же крапива:
как запляшешь тогда? — запоешь!

1996

The reason? A steadfast guard, with
whom you've come to an arrangement,
will sooner or later wave
you in with wide arms. Spring's
resurrection nears:
wintering in heaven's no expense!

I can imagine you, leaping
green to the ground—all around
a blooming meadow outspread.
The same burdock and nettles are
strewn by that footpath. How will
you dance then?—You'll sing!

1996

* * *

Восторгаясь и негодуя,
со своей антикварной лирой,
    мне доставшейся
за гроши на Тишинском рынке,
    беспрепятственно

с вестью по городам и весям,
отдаленным и близлежащим,
    пешешествую; —
браноносных, порфирородных
    повелителей

помянувши недобрым словом,
торопиться вдаль, приближая
    цель стремительно,
всё равно, что стоять на месте
    без движения, —

знаю твердо. — Коль с треском крепкий
ствол преломлен стрелами молний,
    ветвь становится
боковая внезапно главной
    и единственной

жизнестойкой. — Муз кареглазых
я не первый любовник, но и
    не последний же,
чтоб за ними взятым приданым
    бестолково рас-

порядиться и безотчетно,
чтоб запас вотще сокровенный
    слов повыболтать
впопыхах, а там — хоть гори всё
    синим пламенем,

* * *

I'm both enraptured and indignant,
toting my antiquarian lyre—
    old thing I procured
for pennies at Tishinsky market—
    I move with the news

unimpeded from town to village
(both far removed and near as neighbors),
    I foot this distance.
Having once recalled the cerise-clad, spear-
    wielding warriors

with ill-will and thin lip service, then
to hasten into the distance, reel
    the goal actively
closer, this stands in for standing in
    one place, unmoving—

this I know for certain. And when trees
cleave at the crack of lightning's arrow,
    all shattered save one
side branch, this remnant will persist as
    the new cut trunk, so

vigorous. As for the muses, brown-
eyed girls, I'm neither their first lover
    nor yet their last one—
I'm not so dim I'd tie their dowry
    down, then disperse that

prized speech without proper accounting,
some cache I'd vainly blurt away,
    a flurry of word
and then… what? Well, to hell with all that—

как несметных богатств наследник,
обуянный страстями. — Пропасть
не великая
от Гомера до Герострата,
от могущества

до бессилья. — Трущобы строя,
разнесли могильные плиты
с позаброшенных,
мхом поросших кладбищ. — Возводит
и решительно

рушит время, камня на камне
не оставив. — Александрия!
ты, поэзию
между бурь и волнений многих
сохранившая

неизменной, стократ блаженна. —
Оскудели любовь и вера,
лишь надеждою
жив еще человек, обломок
поколения

говорливого бессловесный,
шевеля губами по-рыбьи:
«Если вымести
весь из памяти сор ничтожный,
что останется?»

1998

I'm not heir to their budget-free
trust fund and seized by spending. Still, that
    chasm's not a great
one, between Homer and Herostratus,
    between the mighty

and the meek. In erecting housing
projects, they snatched the last gravestones
    and took them away,
a cemetery's leftovers—moss-
    covered and decayed.

How decisively time erects and
razes, leaving every stone upturned.
    Alexandria!
You who preserved verse through such unrest
    and storm, a hundred

times are you blessed. Still, love and faith
thin quickly, and through hope alone can
    a person live on—
wordless splinter of a garrulous
    generation—one

who'll now wriggle his lips like a fish
gasping for air: "If you sweep all
    your memories clean
of their lingering garbage, what then
    will ever remain?"

1998

Опыт о патриотизме

Князь
Петр Андреевич Вяземский,
наполовину ирландец,
первый президент
Русского исторического общества,
чиновник, придворный, орденоносец,
добрую треть
долгой жизни своей проездивший
по заграницам,
раздраженно брюзжать
возвращался в отчизну время от времени
о народе русском и Боге.

Граф
Толстой Алексей Константинович,
русак чистокровный,
наперсник и друг
детства будущего Царя-освободителя
и сиделец на коленях у Гёте,
редкой силы мужик,
разгибавший подковы, и равнодушный к почестям
в наследных имениях охотник,
в стихах искажал
историю государства российского,
надо всем святым насмехаясь.

О,
какие б им теперь обвинения
предъявили мнимые патриоты,
уличив, например,
в презрении ко всему, чем отечество
справедливо гордится,
в оскорблении чувств
верующих чересчур тщательно,
трепетно и щепетильно, —

Foray into Patriotism

Prince
Pyotr Andreyevich Vyazemsky,
the half-Irish
first president
of the Russian Historical Society,
civil servant, courtier, beribboned with medals,
spent a good third
of his full life traveling
abroad,
but returned to his homeland on occasion
to grouse irascibly
about Russians and God.

Count
Tolstoy, Alexey Konstantinovich,
a true Russian blueblood—
who, in his childhood,
sat on Goethe's lap
and was confidant and friend to the Czar Liberator—
a man of rare strength,
an unbender of horseshoes, unmoved by honors,
hunted on his hereditary estates
but distorted the record
of the Russian nation with his poetry—
he mocked everything holy.

O,
what the so-called patriots
would charge these men with today,
unveiling their disdain
for everything that makes their native land
justly proud,
or how they too reverently,
thoroughly, or rigorously
offended churchgoers' sensibilities;

но, увы, глупцам понять не дано,
ко врагам своим способным только на ненависть,
как они любили Россию!

2013

but alas, it's not the lot of a blockhead—
who's only able to hate enemies—to understand
how these men loved Russia!

2013

«Храм с аркадой»

В Судакской крепости, если от Главных
ворот — налево — до локтя стены —
и вверх, особым на первый праздному
зеваке с виду ничем не приметный,
с торчащего зубом во рту столпа
единственным и с полушарием купола

по-над осьмигранником кратковыйным,
сей дом Господень, куда чередой
в устах отверстых с молитвами мирными
одни за другими, что на берег волны:
из диких нахлынувшие степей
законопослушники Магометовы

петь «Ля илляха илля-Лла» протяжно;
по зыбкому от Лигурийских пучин
пути пришельцы искусствоносные
свой строгий отчетливо «Патэр ностэр»
на мертвом наречии повторять;
со «Шма Исраэль» далекой изгнанники

земли, во всем полагаясь на свиток,
чьи буквы ведомы наперечет;
пространств на суше завоеватели
и на море, «Отче наш» возглашая,
крюкам доверяться и знаменá́м;
простых прямые Мартина грозного

писаний наследники с «Фатэр унзэр»;
единоприродным Вышнего чтя,
из злачных вкруг древней Ноевой пристани
юдолищ выходцы, дабы страстно
«Хайр мэр» твердить и лелеять грусть,
рассудку низкому неподвластную, —

"Temple with an Arcade"

At the Genoese Fortress in Sudak, if you enter
the Main Gate, at the left, and approach the wall's elbow,
then head up from a post—it doesn't strike
the random rubbernecker as much—protruding
like a codger's last tooth, there is a cupola
plopped on a stub-necked octahedron

that glows, a hemisphere's bowl;
this is the Lord's house, where a sequence
of people, lips parted in peaceful prayer,
washes like waves through the door:
see the law-abiding Mahommedans,
flooding in from the wild steppe

to sing "La ilaha illa Allah" in a slow monotone;
see the foreigners hauling their alien art
along the rippled path from the Ligurian Gulf—
they chant their gruff
"Pater Noster" in a language now dead;
or see a distant land's exiles

with their "Sh'ma Israel," who learn
by heart the scroll's trusted marks;
see the conquerors of panoramas
and oceans, who proclaim "Otche Nash" all around,
vesting all hope in hammer and banner;
see the direct heirs of dire Martin

spreading his simple writ, "Vater Unser";
see the fertile vale's natives embracing
Noah's ancient haven, Monophysites
honoring the Most High, each one
ardently affirming "Hayr Mer," each cherishing
a grief sadder than low intellect can know...

все были некогда здесь, а ныне —
в открытый с восьми до восьми музей,
где фрески, михраб и разноязычные
по стенам надписи, вход свободный,
и внемлет мольбам одинаково Бог
всего разобщенного человечества.

2005—2008

all of them once traveled here, but now—
a free museum that's open eight to eight,
where polyglot inscriptions intermix
with frescoes and the mihrab, where God
hears, with equal heed, entreaties
from all the fractured hosts of Man.

2005 – 2008

*   *   *

Олегу Чухонцеву

Стальночешуйчатый, крылатый,
Серпокохтистый, двурогатый…
Г. Державин

Зверь огнедышущий с пышною гривой,
серпокогтистый, твой норов игривый
не понаслышке знаком
всем, кто, вдыхая гниения запах,
некогда мызган в чешуйчатых лапах,
лизан стальным языком,

дважды раздвоенным, всем, кто копытом
бит по зубам и пером ядовитым
колот и глажен не раз
больно и нежно, кто чувствовал близко
испепеляющего Василиска
взгляд немигающих глаз,

взгляд на себе. — Никаких предисловий,
лишь заохотится мяса и крови,
зев отверзается твой
и наполняется плотью утроба
плотно с причмоком, — навыкате оба
только не сыты жратвой

ока; бывает: ни рылом, ни ухом
не поведет, расстилается пухом,
кротко виляя хвостом. —
О Государство! не ты ли? — Повадки,
взлет ли стремя, пребывая ль в упадке,
те же, что в изверге том, —

*   *   *

for Oleg Chukhontsev

Steely-scaled, winged,
Sickle-clawed, horned…
Gavriil Derzhavin

Fire-breathing beast, fumes wreathing your figure,
with sickle-claws clenched your playful nature
is clear: an open book
read by all who've caught the whiff of ruin
as they're clamped in those glittering talons,
the skin on their backs

raked by your steel-file tongue; or who've taken
hooves in the teeth, been stabbed with a poison
pen; or who've realized
(too late) that they're in too deep; or whose gaze
has met the basilisk's, his deadly rays
loosed from unblinking eyes.

Eyes were all they saw. You gave no prelude,
cutting right to the kill, feasting on blood.
Your gruesome maw opens—
you glut your fetid gut, you slake your dry
gullet, slurping, smacking, rolling your eyes
in satisfaction

with your meal and something more… though fodder
is what I have plainly watched you offer—
not slaughter—to the lambs.
O State! Is this you? Whether you're planing
new heights or wallowing in your waning,
that leviathan

разницы нет никакой. Поневоле
тыщами слизью набитых: «Доколе!» —
во всеуслышанье ртов
жертвы б во чреве твоем провещали.
(— Если тебе не хватает печали,
я поделиться готов.)

1998

and you share these traits. Thousands of victims
would cry "Enough!" from your belly's cistern,
          their voices thick and phlegm-
filled for all who've ears to hear. They have to.
(*I bear these woes and more. If you've too few,*
          I'll gladly share them.)

1998

* * *

Языком эзоповым не владея,
потому что поздно учить язык,
нечестивца, вора или злодея
власть имущих — собственными привык
называть именами без оговорок,
невзирая на звания и чины,
сопричастности не деля на сорок,
не преувеличивая вины.

Обходи меня стороной, прохожий!
ибо только ноги тебя спасут, —
нет, не человечий на них, но Божий
постоянно я призываю суд,
где защитник и обвинитель слиты
воедино, свидетель — и тот один,
пламенеют гневом Его ланиты,
свет сияет истины от седин.

Я со древа страха земного зерен
не вкушал и не пил боязни вод
кесарю назло, как бы ни был черен
или бел, — иным наполнял живот,
посему, дрожащий, как можно прытче
от меня беги, не жалея пят,
а не то, напялив личины притчи,
за спиною хищники засопят.

2001

* * *

The language of Aesop eludes me,
and it's too late to be taught a new tongue;
whether they're villains, reprobates, or robbers,
I'm used to calling the powers
that be—with no provisos, no thought
for rank or title—by their actual names.
I won't thin complicity among the many,
or inflate an individual shame.

Passer-by, be advised: give me a wide berth!
Only your feet now can save you.
For it is not the earth's verdict
I'm calling down here—it is God's.
When the defense and D.A. conspire
together, one witness gathers Himself
to judge: see His face flame with righteous ire,
see His robes effulgent with truth.

From the tree of earthly fear I eat no seeds,
from the waters of fright I've not drunk,
for this is Caesar's portion I spurn.
I've filled my belly with other things.
So you, little whimperer, flee now!
Hightail it out of here, make haste,
lest animals swathed in sermon silk attack.
Your heels will feel the hot breath of beasts.

2001

IV.

Катавасия на Фоминой неделе

Gratia cum Nymphis geminisque sororibus audet
ducere nuda choros.
Immortalia ne speres monet annus, et almum
qua rapit hora diem.

[Грация хоровод в окружении Нимф и сестричек
стала нагая водить.
Вечной жизни не жди, — и год убеждает, и каждый
время ворующий день.]
Q. Horatius Flaccus, Od., IV, 7

Но нет! — он может пробудиться,
Из гроба света луч пролить.
Граф Д. И. Хвостов.
К Дарье Алексеевне Державиной
на Паше, 1816 года Июля 16 дня

Подражание Хвостову
сочинить ко дню Христову
не случилось, — на Страстной
строчки — чаяния паче —
для решения задачи
сей не влезло ни одной

в голову. — Привычка к лаврам
быстро делает кентавром,
грозным с виду, косным в шаг, —
к вящей славе Их Сиятельств
в нарушенье обязательств
не стоится на ушах,

на потеху следопытам
не летается, копытом
стройно в воздухе маша:
раз-два-три, два-три-четыре. —

Katabasia for St. Thomas Week

Gratia cum Nymphis geminisque sororibus audet
ducere nuda choros.
Immortalia ne speres, monet annus et almum
quae rapit hora diem.

[*The Graces and their twins the nymphs will dare*
to dance undressed.
Don't hope for immortality. The year gives warning,
each hour steals the day's sweet life.]
Horace, *Odes* IV. 7

But no! He may awaken
and send a ray of light from out his coffin.
Count D. I. Khvostov,
to Darya Alekseyevna Derzhavina,
on the Pasha, the 16th day of July, 1816

I couldn't quite compose an homage
to Count Khvostov in time for Christmas,
not as I'd meant to, not a line—
despite my hopes for Holy Week.
I've yet to solve this simple problem,
and no solution comes to mind.

The moment you take praise for granted
is the moment you become a centaur:
crooked of gait, a grim demeanor.
But I'll not tie myself in knots,
neglecting my own obligations,
just to win Their Lordships more honor.

Nor shall I fly to tease my trackers,
my slender hoof held up to mark
the time I've spent in graceful flight:
one-two-three, *two*-three-four.

Неприкаянная в мире
дольнем странствует душа,

тяжкий груз таская тела,
от известного предела
неизведанного до, —
с миром выспренним в разлуке
не сидит, поджавши руки,
в ожидании Го— Do— .

В ожидании чего-то
эдакого: поворота,
перемены невзначай, —
изменив порядок строчек,
память вырвала листочек
с приглашением на чай.

Старое стихотворенье,
что прокисшее варенье,
крытый плесенью пирог. —
Не для всех своих исчадий
остается добрым дядей
вдохновений светлый бог.

Страх и ужас: вот бы если
всё умершие воскресли
без разбору, — что тогда? —
Понесутся целым скопом
по америкам, европам
в залу Страшного суда,

друг отталкивая друга,
точно вихорь или вьюга,
всё сметая на пути,
необузданны и дики,
оглушительные крики
сея: «Не развоплоти!» —

My restless soul still wanders across
the earthly world's endless sights;

it drags my body's heavy load,
testing the limits of where we go
into the known and unexplored.
My soul won't sit on its hands and wait—
off by itself in its lofty world—
for the Second Coming of the Lord.

For that certain something I'd heard,
I wait; for a turn of fate that's better,
a sea change or serendipity...
my memory has switched some lines
and found, stuck between the mind's
pages, an invitation out to tea.

A poem that's old is like a pie
encrusted with mold, a sour jam
that sports a furry rind.
Likewise the god of inspiration,
who'll only shine on his chosen brood.
To others he's wholly unkind.

Fear and horror: what if the dead
were reincarnated, willy-nilly?
Could we handle them all?
I see the herds stampede across
the Europes and the Americas—
they enter the Day of Judgment's halls.

Jostling each other out of the way,
they move like snowstorms or squalls
that clear all paths of debris—
they're wild and unrestrained, their screams
can scatter us all with this deafening plea:
"Don't unembody me!"

«Пощади меня, Всевышний!» —
«И меня!» — «И я не лишний!» —
взвоют все до одного. —
Милосерд Господь и правед, —
только избранных восставит
или — лучше — никого.

Никого. — Какая демо-
кратия! — Моя поэма,
совершая трудный путь,
чертит странные зигзаги. —
Хорошо б у тихой влаги
на припеке отдохнуть:

«Мне ли, жителю вселенной,
внятен будет современный
шепот, ропот или вой?» —
Ясные бросая взгляды,
плотоядные Наяды
плещут вешнею водой. —

Всяк родженный не однажды
глада не страшится, жажды,
обстоятельств или нужд,
хоть в казарме, хоть на зоне
размышляет о Назоне,
человеческого чужд. —

То, что свойственно природе,
тще не тщись в угоду моде
изменить, — со что и как,
как ни силься, что ни делай:
день взлетел, как ангел белый,
пал, что черный демон, мрак. —

Сутки — прочь, вторые сутки
помрачение в рассудке. —
Кто мне толком объяснит? —

"Have pity on me, Almighty! Spare me!"
"And me!" "And me! I matter too!"
they wail in unison.
The Lord is merciful and just:
he'll only raise a chosen few,
or—even better—none.

None. Now *that's* dim-
ocracy. My own epic poem
traces out its funny zig-zags
as it travels its difficult path.
How nice it'd be to laze near water,
soak up the rays and just relax.

"Will this newfangled whispering, grumbling,
and howling ever make sense to me:
the Universe's denizen?"
The flesh-eating Naiads shoot me glances—
they splash their vernal water coyly
and flirt in my direction.

Whoever's been born has felt the pangs
of thirst or hunger more than once.
He's been resigned to poverty.
Even in barracks or labor camps,
where all that is human is foreign,
he ponder Ovid's poetry.

So don't exert yourself to change
the native and natural order of things,
to fit today's modish fashion.
Your *like* and *as* are wholly futile:
the dawn rose like a white angel,
the darkness fell, black as a demon.

I've lost one day and then a second
to this growing eclipse of my reason.
Where's the answer coming from

Четкий на вопрос вопросов
даст ответ? — Какой философ? —
Но молчат и Фет, и Ф. И. Т.

(псевдоним, инициалы). —
Геркулес у ног Омфалы,
весь в оборках кружевных,
северянинскому пажу
подражая, сучит пряжу,
упорядочен и тих.

Он, от жизни голубиной
отмахнувшийся дубиной,
облачится в шкуру льва
и взойдет на склоны неба
убеждаться в том, что Геба
девственная, чем вдова

безутешная, не хуже, —
тоже думает о муже:
«Я — невеста, ты — жених,
ты — жених, а я — невеста». —
Нет ни времени, ни места
на подробности про них.

Так болтать шутливым слогом
можно долго и о многом:
то Ерема, то Фома, —
слов — полно, да толку мало, —
мысль, увы, не ночевала
в недрах некошна ума. —

«Кто герой моей поэмы? —
Я ль один? — А может, все мы,
кто не низок, не высок,
у кого, хотя негромкий,
свой, отдельный — там потомки
разберутся — голосок?» —

to this question of questions?
Which thinker's got a clear solution?
Both Fet and F. I. T. are mum.

(Of course: a pseudonym, initials.)
Here's Hercules in flounces lacey—
he sits at fierce Omphale's feet.
He's just like Severyanin's page-boy.
The hero spins his yarn effetely,
so dutiful, mute, and meek.

But with a swing of oaken club
our Hercules undoes his dovecote.
Again arrayed in lion skin,
he soon ascends the vault of heaven
to locate Hebe virginal.
Zeus's daughter is akin

to widows inconsolable:
like them, she wants a husband too.
"I'm the bride, you're my bridegroom.
You're the bridegroom; I'm your bride."
Further details, though, are moot.
I've no more time to talk, nor room.

We joke like this in endless cycles
but to what end? Take Jeremiah,
Thomas, or any of their kind:
they're rich in words, but what's their use
if thought, alas, won't tread a path
through a reader's unmown mind?

"Who is the hero of this poem?
Just me alone? Or all of us?
Whoever's neither prince nor lout?
Whoever's got a singular voice,
however hushed? Let the generations
to follow figure it out."

В гневе огненной геенны,
ненависть! не лезь на стены,
укроти свой, зависть! пыл,
не скрипи зубами, злоба! —
Да, Державин встал из гроба
и меня благословил. —

Смерти нет — одна морока:
классицизм или барокко? —
Зримый мир и мир иной
связаны, перетекая, —
катавасия такая
на неделе Фоминой.

1999—2002

O Hate! Don't climb the walls inside
fiery Gehenna's hellish wrath!
And calm your ardor, Envy!
Spite, you shouldn't grind your teeth.
Yes, Derzhavin has finally risen
from his grave to bless me.

There is no death, but there is this mess:
is it Classical or just Baroque?
The world we see and the world we seek
are linked and bound to intermingle.
Behold: my katabasia
in honor of St. Thomas Week.

1999 – 2002

* * *

Эти бездонные ночи в июле,
О![1]
Ты вопрошаешь: — Меня обманули?
— Да, — отвечаю, — но как!

Лучше не спрашивай. Долго во власти
сам обаяния их
я находился, и на тебе, здрасьте, —
проза испортила стих.

1997—1998

[1] Восклицательный знак.

*   *   *

These nights that won't wear out in July,
        O my![1]
(And yet you ask: *'twas all just a lie?*
        Indeed, but a great one!)

You ask? Please don't. How long now I've lived
        in awe they'd bestowed,
when quickly—hello! here you go!—pfft!
        The poem fell to prose.

1997 – 1998

[1] To be pronounced: "O my, exclamation!"

V.

*   *   *

Поспешим
стол небогатый украсить
помидорами алыми,
петрушкой кучерявой и укропом,

чесноком,
перцем душистым и луком,
огурцами в пупырышках
и дольками арбузными. — Пусть масло,

как янтарь
солнца под оком, возблещет
ослепительно. — Черного
пора нарезать хлеба, белой соли,

не скупясь,
выставить целую склянку. —
Виноградного полная
бутыль не помешает. — Коль приятно

утолять
голод и жажду со вкусом! —
Наступающей осени
на милость не сдадимся, не сдадимся

ни за что. —
Всесотворившему Богу
озорные любовники
угрюмых ненавистников любезней.

1992, 2000

* * *

Let's hurry
to grace this meager table
with red tomatoes
and stacks of melon wedges,

with onions
and dill, with parsley and peppers,
with garlic and goose-pimpled
cucumbers. Let the oil,

resplendent
as sunlit amber, glimmer.
It's time to slice
black bread, to strew salt

lavishly.
Let's offer bottles full
of wine and tipple
till they're gone. How pleasant

to placate
our palates and sup with taste!
We won't give up,
we won't give in to autumn,

not a bit.
For God, the Creator of All,
likes naughty lovers
far more than dreary doubters.

1992, 2000

* * *

Насыщение, а не вкус,
о котором водит Француз
неустанно четыре века
языком по полости рта! —
Вся премудрость его пуста
для голодного человека!

Мельтешения скудных блюд
не приемлет привычный люд
к изобилию щей да каши;
нет урчания в животе —
можно думать о красоте:
насыщение — счастье наше!

Преуспеет в словесном тот
ремесле, кто туго набьет
отощавшему снедью пузо, —
чем богата, всё из печи
с пылу с жару на стол мечи,
да поболе, русская Муза!

2003—2007

* * *

Satiety prevails, not taste,
despite the Frenchman's discerning mouth.
At least four centuries he's spent
loving taste, urbane and proud.
Still, his subtleties prove paltry
to any man who's hungry.

The normal folk just don't prefer
small plates arrayed until they're dizzy
in lieu of lots of soup and porridge.
It's easier to stomach beauty
when your stomach fills your vest:
satiety is our happiness!

The one who stuffs these folks with pap,
fills 'em up and staves off hunger,
will soon excel in verbal craft.
So empty your fridge, unload your larder,
cook up the contents however you choose—
just don't be stingy, Russian muse!

2003 – 2007

* * *

Циклопов язык из одних согласных:
шипящих, сопящих, небных, губных,
гортанных, — меж древлезвонкопрекрасных
ему не затеряться. На них

восславить лепо сребро потока,
волос любимой нощную ткань,
пропеть про *грустно и одиноко*,
земли и неба звенея брань

и чаши с горьким питьем. А этим,
как око единым на голом лбу,
сродни изрыгать проклятья столетьям
и всей вселенной трубить судьбу.

Нет равных ему в наречиях дольних,
безгласному, — люди на нем молчат.
Заткнись и ты, мой болтливый дольник, —
язык циклопов суров и свят!

1992—1994

* * *

Cyclopean language consists of consonants:
palatals, labials, sniveling sibilants,
and glottals. It will never be confused
for the sonorous lilts of the ancients.

In those it's meet to praise silvern streams
and lover's hair woven with starlit evenings,
or to sing *sadness and mourning*,
the fierce battles of earth and heaven,

cups with bitter drafts. But this tongue,
just like a lone eye lodged in a forehead,
is fit for spitting curses at the ages,
blaring your fate to the cosmos like a trumpet.

In all the lowland dialects it is unequalled,
voiceless; in it people keep quiet.
And you, my garrulous dol'nik, shut up too!
Cyclopean speech is stern and sacred.

1992 – 1994

* * *

Сложного сложнее, простого проще,
то неповоротлива, то шустра,
громоздясь на горы, врываясь в рощи,
языками яростными костра
ласково крутя, шевеля глумливо,
рушится стремительная с обрыва
и встает целехонька, как ни в чем
не бывало, плотная и сквозная,
сведуща во всем, ничего не зная,
собственным себя подопря плечом.

Сопредельным странам грозя набегом,
мир даруя прочим издалека,
Ноевым взлетающая ковчегом
над водой под самые облака,
раздается вширь обоюдокрыла,
весть о том, что будет и есть и было,
претворить пытается в кровь и плоть
всех существ, замешанных на соблазнах,
потому что в лицах и видах разных
праведную любит ее Господь.

2002

*   *   *

Harder than hard and simpler than simple,
it stumbles at times, but can be nimble.
It climbs a mountain, it drops
into a wooded copse. It mumbles
forlornly, then babbles brightly
with a tongue as mad as a bonfire's flame.
It crashes off a cliff like a boulder
but pops up good as new and toughened.
It's both an expert and a know-nothing.
It props itself up on its own shoulder.

It threatens contiguous countries
and grants peace to the rest from afar.
Like Noah's Ark it crests the waves
now risen sky-high, then starts to soar
on double-edged wings, spreading ever wider.
It tries to turn the Good News of all
that is, will be, or was, into the blood
that flows through every craving creature,
because—in all its facets and features—
it is the righteous one the Lord has loved.

2002

* * *

Сирень отцвела, распустился жасмин
    на Малой Никитской и Бронной, —
единство враждующих двух половин,
    в себя безответно влюбленный,
шагами я меряю улиц пустых
    пространство, ступая сторожко, —
вдруг под ноги шмыг, раздвоивши стих,
    сомнения черная кошка.

В какой-то успел переулок едва
    свернуть я, как всё изменилось:
пожухла трава и опала листва,
    поземкой зима зазмеилась,
навстречу киша повалила толпа,
    Москва переехала в Питер, —
и хладной рукой с горячего лба
    я пот лихорадочно вытер.

1996—1998

* * *

The lilac has faded, the jasmine's begun to bloom
        on Little Nikitskaya and Bronnaya avenues;
I'm glue that holds two warring halves,
        I suffer from a self-love unfulfilled.
I measure the space in empty streets,
        marking my paces warily…
When *whoosh!* the black cat of doubt flashes at my feet—
        he slices my poem in two.

I barely had time to turn down a lane
        when suddenly everything changes.
The leaves are down, the grass brown and bare,
        the wind wraps winter everywhere,
and a teeming mob swarms toward me—
        Moscow moved to St. Petersburg.
I take a cool hand to my hot brow
        and wipe the sweat off, feverishly.

1996 – 1998

Запоздалая ода Екатрине Великой, Императрице и Самодержице Всероссийской, при воззрении на зыбкое отражение в луже памятника Ея, что на Невском проспекте в Санкт-Петербурге, декабрьским вечером 2006 года

Тебе,
царице
северной
сей
державы,
дерзну ли хвалу
вознести после стольких
величия полных певцов,
уже до меня всё награды,
всю славу себе стяжавших?
Ни перстней, ни табакерок,
усыпанных алмазами, не жду!
Легко воспевать и выгодно
живых, сребра и злата от них,
высоких чинов и званий взыскуя,
верный доход сулящих владельцу
имений, и прочих благ и стяжаний,
устойчивых и непреложных! Любой
певец о том помышляет с надеждой
тайной иль явной, но обоснованной.
Суд над правителями посмертный
вершат беспристрастные летописцы,
дабы всё по своим расставить местам
и должное всем воздать:
кто выспрь возлетел воздушным шаром,
кому упасть случилось ниже некуда,
чья кровь пролилась безвинно, чей сдавленный
в горле затих крик, на свободу так и не вырвавшись,
лепет любовный кого за ступенью ступень
по шаткой лестнице взомчал до верху самого,
откуда весь мир, возможный и зримый
как на ладони зерно конопляное видится,
о ком сперва безмолвствовать, потом рассказывать
повелено было на каждом углу, наоборот ли,
переставив наречия временны́е. Лиц и событий

истинная соразмерность при помощи
увеличительных и уменьшительных стекол
выявляется всенепременно. Мне же,
не летописцу, но певцу позднорожденному,
по созвучию научившемуся слова подбирать
и по мере укладывать, строй и порядок, предписанный
сводом правил неколебимых, безжалостно и хладнокровно
разрушающему, ради создания и утверждения новых,
свой приговор выносить издалека не пристало. В защиту
повелительницы премудрой части моря и суши той,
от которой и нынешний сколок иль клок, после всех переделов
оставшийся, зрится немыслимым и восприятия чувственного
за гранью находящимся, немстительной ко врагам быть желавшей,
справедливой ко подданным и милостивой, насколько возможно,
здесь и сейчас воздвигается, Екатерина! речь непредвзятая мной.
О могущественная владычица, окруженная сонмом великолепных
мужей и жен, заставивших трубы и лиры согласно звучать повсюду,
ибо только достойным достойные служат честно! Се непроглоченный
львом пучинным в лесу щегловитом, се луне надломивший рога, се хищных
птиц всех мастей ощипыватель догола, се мира заключитель долгожданного,
се бесстрашный по лужам соленым ходок, се счастливый разитель во бранном
поле и на ложе, се державной реки воспитатель, се расплодительница мысленных
стад и чувственных стай, се деяний свершенных и подвигов отдаленным потомкам
возвеститель правдивый в творениях стройных, премудрый свидетель и соучастник
великих событий, поскольку вне таковых речетворческий дар не вполне раскрывается.
Ничтожен пиит, коль на долю его прозябание выпало при бездарных и недальновидных
властителях, окруженных алчной сворою и ненасытной. Что ему остается? Дышать
равномерно дыханием прежде дышавших и с тихой тоскою смотреть обреченно
на искаженное отражение памятника твоего, самодержица, в мутном
декабрьском зерцале, поразительно напоминающем рваными
очертаниями своими нечто знакомое с детства: карту ль,
на которую ставить нельзя, медведицу ли большую,
семизвездием блещущую бесстрастно
сквозь пространство
и время.

2006—2010

Belated Ode to Catherine the Great, Empress and Autocratrice of All Russia, Upon Gazing into a Puddle on a December Evening in 2006 and Seeing the Rippling Reflection of Her Monument on Nevsky Prospect in St. Petersburg

Is it you,
Tsarina
of this
Northern
power,
to whom I dare raise up
my exaltation, singing after
so many singers richly praised
have already won, long before me,
prizes and glory for themselves?
I don't expect one signet ring
or diamond snuff-box for myself!
It's easy to celebrate the living
and it's lucrative to accrue their gold and silver,
the ranks and titles they offer,
the estates that promise a steady income
for their owners, or other acquisitions and blessings,
each so stable and secure! Any
singer has thought of this or hoped for it,
privately or overtly… either way they're justified.
But it's only the chroniclers impartial
who pass a posthumous judgment on leaders,
a way to put them in their proper place
and deliver to each what's due:
who ascended skyward like a loose balloon;
who chanced to fall so low none could sink lower;
whose blameless blood was wrongly spilled; whose strangled cry
died in his throat, never fleeing toward freedom;
whose lover's prattle raced step by step
up a creaking staircase, until it reached the topmost
landing from which the world can be surveyed,
a world as visible and potent as a hemp seed in an open hand;
about whom the rest were told they must be silent, then forced
to talk on every corner; about whom the inverse
was true, just switch the sequence of commands.

People's deeds and truest measure—with help
from history's varied lenses—will be
ascertained without fail. But that work doesn't fit me.
I'm not so much a chronicler as a late-born singer
who's learned to choose his words by consonance
and lay them down in proper measure; nor am I the one—
cold-blooded and pitiless—who'd destroy the system prescribed
by code of law, then ratify another I liked better. It's not my place
to render judgment from afar. So in defense of the sovereign
who wisely ruled that part of land and sea of which the current
nation's but a copy, a shred or tatter persisting after
many repartitions, a mote beyond the pale
of what our senses can apprehend—and in defense of she who deigns to forgo
vengeance against her enemies, she who's just and merciful to all her subjects—
for Catherine, here and now! I've engineered this impartial speech.
O mighty lady! O sovereign surrounded by a crowd of men and women
magnificent! They've compelled trumpets and lyres to harmonize everywhere,
for only the worthy ought convene around a worthy Queen. Behold: a man undrowned by Swedish sailors,
their lion no match for his forest of masts; another snapped the Turkish crescent's horns.
Here's one who plucked the feathers off state birds, both large and small, while this one made a needed peace;
here's the man who conquered salty puddles; and here's the happy victor both of battles
and of bedsheets. Here's the teacher of her Majesty's young, strong river; here's the woman who
bred herds of thought and flocks of sensibility. And here's the righteous herald of deeds,
whose dulcet works will speak to our descendants. All are witnesses
of monumental times (without which the gift of speech will fail to reach fruition).
Worthless the poet whose lot it is to vegetate beneath improvident and feeble
masters, surrounded by a greedy, insatiable crew. What's left to him? To breathe
evenly with those who breathed before, to gaze—with silent sadness, doomed—
at your monument, O Autocratrice, distorted in this December
looking-glass, all overcast, its rippling edges calling to mind
something I knew back in childhood: maybe a card
a fool alone would bet on, maybe the Big Dipper,
its seven stars shining impassively
through space
and time.

2006 – 2010

Памяти Восточной Пруссии

Андрею Виноградову

I

Здесь всё чужое: аисты на гнездах,
привычкой занесенные сюда,
обычная земля, обычный воздух,
    обычная вода.

Сотворены другим каким-то богом
и небеса, и дольние поля,
и солнце, по извилистым дорогам
    пылящее, паля.

Здесь петухи поют не так, не этак
кузнечики стрекочут, странен скрип
густой листвой отягощенных веток
    дубов, берез и лип.

Основанный воинственным тевтоном
старинный замок — череп восковой,
как ни тоскуй о безвременьи оном,
    не станет головой.

Всего, что зримо мне и что незримо,
таинственный закон непостижим, —
так варвару среди развалин Рима
    казалось всё чужим.

II

Язык руин не внятен:
ливон не вышел вон, —
немало белых пятен
легло на черный фон.

In Memory of East Prussia

for Andrey Vinogradov

I

Everything here's alien: storks in their nests—
habit led each one here—
the everyday earth, the air's everyday breath,
        the everyday water.

Formed by some separate kind of god
there's this heaven, the fields sliced just
right, and a sun to scorch these winding roads
        and kick up their dust.

Here the roosters sing off key, crickets
chirr improperly, and strange is the screech
of foliage, growing thickest
        on oak, lime, or birch branch.

Built by bellicose Teutons,
an antique castle's a cast-wax skull.
However much its emptiness saddens
        you, it'll never again be full.

Of everything around me, seen and unseen, the one
deep law cannot be known—
so too did barbarians, astride Rome's ruins,
        think everything alien.

II

The ruin's tongue is unintelligible:
the Livonian's no longer around—
these countless lacunae stand out,
bright against the black background.

Проступят из-под краски
и надпись и чертеж, —
трагической развязки
дождешься — ждешь не ждешь.

Стоит на пьедестале
осиротелом тень;
в подробности, в детали
вникать, вдаваться лень.

Затянет паутина
зерцало озерца,
но матери без сына,
что сыну без отца.

III

«О том, что мы когда-нибудь умрем,
деревья здесь рыдали янтарем,
когда еще ничто не предвещало,
что вызванные из небытия
велением Господним — ты и я —
сберемся жить... » — Элегии начало

оборвано, — ее продлить, увы!
нет вдохновения, из головы
не тщусь тянуть по строчке и подавно,
пока выносит на берег волна,
курчавая наследница руна
златого, плач окаменелый плавно.

IV

Полшестого на проржавелом
циферблате который год, —
    время выбыло.

Both first sketch and final signature
emerge from under the paint—
sad denouement that hunts
you out, no matter what you want.

On the orphaned pedestal
falls a lone shadow;
There are finer points and details
we're too lazy to dig through.

Cobwebs now cover
the pond's dusty mirror;
as a mother mourns her sons,
so the sons their father.

III

"As for the truth that one day we'll die,
the trees here wept clear amber,
back when nothing yet could portend
that those called out—i.e. you and I—
from the dark ether on God's orders
would suit up for living..." The elegy's begin-

ing is severed—but to prolong it, ah!
my head's inspiration-less,
and I've not endeavored to drag line after line
for some time now. Gently a wave—
the Golden Fleece's curly heiress—
floats the fossilized tears to the coastline.

IV

For how many years has this clock-
face's 5:30 been rusted fast—
            time's left the station.

Летописец! углем и мелом
дни, со лба утирая пот,
    ибо выбора

нет, прилежнее отмечай-ка,
не пытаясь понять, внемли
    завещаньице, —
то приветствует криком чайка
всё, что в землю иль из земли
    возвращается.

V

Усеяны густо зубами дракона
песчаные горы на Куршской косе,
делящей бурливое надвое лоно
упругого моря, — усеяны все.

В урочное время по всем косогорам,
разбужены распрей, они прорастут,
согбенными соснами встав под напором
стихии безумной, — останутся тут

полоскою леса, угрюмой и хмурой.
Так было, так будет, — из жара да в дрожь
при мысли: на них несуразной фигурой,
на прошлых и будущих, сам я похож.

VI

Мост, ведущий в никуда
    чрез ручей смердящий:
говорливая вода
    притворилась спящей.

Chronicler! Take up your coal and chalk
to mark the day more attentively. Dab your brow sweat.
            All other options

elude you. So quickly now, note this
little testament—just take it down, don't
            try to fathom it.
For the seagull's shrill voice
greets everything that's in the earth, or
            by the earth begot.

V

The sandy hills of the Curonian Spit,
seeded with dragon's teeth, cleave
the sea's elastic lap in two turbulent
halves; the Spit's been seeded.

As usual the men arose bristling.
They awoke to discord, then strained
to straighten, like gnarled pines striving
against the frenzied elements; now they remain,

a thin strip of woods, overcast and sullen.
So it was, and so it shall be.
My blood freezes; I realize we're kin.
I too was sown senselessly.

VI

A bridge, nowhere-bound,
    spans a loathsome stream;
the waters ceased their babble,
    feigning lethargy.

Ни тропинки никакой,
   ибо жребий брошен, —
луг, уверенной рукой
   времени не кошен.

В праздник там, на том лугу,
   веселятся тени,
разбивая на бегу
   чашечки растений.

Память и забвенье — два
   берега — едины:
мост не перейден едва
   мной до середины.

VII

Старый фотограф с треножником из дюрали
бродит по пляжу тщетно в поисках тех,
кто пожелал бы снимок на фоне дали
Бельта ли, гор ли песчаных, но — как на грех —

никого: никому ничего не надо, —
отдыхающих тыщи снабжены
кодаками, поляроидами — не досада
неимоверной, но сожаление — глубины.

Бос, молчалив, минуя свалку людскую,
он по песку одной, по волне другой,
полон тоской, которой и я тоскую,
не оставляя следов, ступает ногой.

Из сыновей приемных златого Феба
самый последний — самый любимый ты!
брось свой треножник, фотографируй небо,
море и солнце, блещущее с высоты.

1997

Not a single trail remains
    since there's nothing to decide.
This spreading meadow's still green,
    uncut by time's sure scythe.

The shades take their leisure
    with picnics in that vale;
wherever they gambol
    they trample spring petals.

Memory and oblivion—two
    shores—make one.
I've not crossed the bridge,
    but linger in-between.

VII

An old photographer wanders, aluminum
tripod in tow, raking the beach vainly for one
who'd wish herself pictured against a horizon
of belted pines or crags of sand, but—as if to spite him—

no one's to be found; nobody needs anything—
not the countless tourists, each equipped
with Polaroids and Kodaks—and it's no staggering
aggravation, though regret, nonetheless, seeps

in. Shoeless, taciturn, he passes the trash-heaps
of people, dividing his feet between sand and surf.
He's filled with sorrow, which is my sorrow,
leaving no tracks as he goes forth.

Of all gilded Apollo's adopted sons
surely you're the last and most beloved!
Abandon that tripod and photograph heaven—
the sea, the sun, radiating from its altitude!

1997

Надпись над дверями тбилисской бани

Смертных сердца прожигая глаголом
иль услаждая божественный слух
вычурной речью, я помню, что голым
вышел на свет, не стыдясь повитух.

Случай мне вновь без смущенья и срама,
словно пред Богом, по долгом посте,
кающемуся под сводами храма,
выпал явиться во всей наготе.

Серная бани тбилисской утроба
каждого может, отмыв добела,
Лазарем сделать, восставшим из гроба,
или младенцем в чем мать родила.

Банщик сотрет рукавицей овечьей
грязь, что в скудельный впиталась сосуд,
подлинный облик вернув человечий, —
страшный не страшен здесь бывшему суд.

Господи, так же очистить и душу
дай до вселения в общий Твой дом! —
с ней разлучения тела я трушу,
вечную жизнь представляя с трудом.

2013

Inscription over the Entrance to a Tbilisi Banya

Now that I've burnt the human heart with words
or pleased celestial ears with all I've rhapsodized,
I can remember how I entered this world:
au naturel and bold before the midwives.

But here's the chance again—without a scrap
of shame or chagrin, as if my God had viewed
my fast or heard my every penitent word
inside the arched cathedral—to strut out nude.

The Tbilisi banya's brimstone womb
can turn a man—fresh-scrubbed, free of soot,
and cleansed of sin—into a Lazarus
or newborn who's just donned his birthday suit.

The banya man then wields his sheepskin mitten,
scouring me until I'm clean as a whistle.
No need to fear the Judgment from in here,
all stains erased right off your pauper's vessel.

Lord, before I move into Your house divine,
please let me cleanse my soul like this!
Once it's left my body, what happens next?
Eternal life is hard to fathom, I admit.

2013

* * *

Не я ли прежде безжалостным
захватчиком отвоевывал
у пенной пучины сушу,
чтоб можно, сверша священный
обряд, на почву мне твердую
стопы, не ведая страха

животного, было выставить? —
Закончены кроволитные
бои до срока, — пора бы
пересчитать поголовно
победы и поражения,
вничью или в чью-то пользу,

случайно или намеренно:
и с лицевой и с изнаночной
едина ткань, обращаясь
обеими сторонами! —
Но все-таки, как ни выверни,
я создал плавучий остров,

одновременно и движимый
и неподвижный, — откуда бы
ветра ни дули, своими
путями ему стремиться
и, ширясь, нести растительность
обильную выспрь. — А ныне

рачительному хозяину
он стал велик, и границами
раздвигся так, что пределов
уже не окинуть оком,
да не послужат помехою
ни сны дурные, ни вести:

* * *

Wasn't I the man who seized
dry land from frothy sea,
one more hard-hearted invader?
And didn't I achieve this feat
to discharge my holy rites and set
my feet on solid ground,

no more to feel animal fear.
The bloody fighting has finished
early; it's time again to count
the banners won and lost,
to take stock of draws
and drawn-out battles,

what's gained by fluke and what's
hard-fought. (Just flip the cloth:
it's still the same when seen
from either front or back!)
Still, no matter how you twist
the tale, I built a floating island,

it's mobile and immobile;
the wind may blow this way
or that, and yet it follows
its own path, growing wider,
its vegetative burden
ever higher. But now

the island's bigger than its
painstaking owner can handle.
It's grown so wide you cannot
cast an eye and spy its many
shores, not anymore. And neither
nightmares or news can block it.

достаточно обустроены
все грады его и веси все,
все пристани, все дороги,
и храмины, и кладбища, —
открывший свою Америку
не зарится на чужую.

Что делать с огромным островом,
без ведома прирастающим? —
Довольно и половины
для жизни его владельцу, —
берите всё, что приглянется,
и делайте что хотите.

2002

It's so finely apportioned:
replete with cities and scales,
with wharves and roads, with all
its cemeteries and structures.
Whoever finds his own New World
won't covet another's old one.

What's to be done with my island,
massive now and growing daily?
Half is more than enough
for its master to live on.
Take what catches your eye
and do with it what you will.

2002

*   *   *

Сын промысла, поверя сметы,
Речет: пророчу час кометы.
Граф Хвостов

Гневной богини ожившая статуя,
светлая вестница зла!
Что ты еще предвещаешь, хвостатая?
что на хвосте принесла?
Чем ты — невзгодами, скорбями, голодом —
неотразимо грозишь?

Хладная льдина в огне Гераклитовой
непримиримой борьбы!
Не сомневайся, стыда не испытывай —
в стылую землю гробы
сей, и дождутся на поле неполотом
всходов медведка да мышь.

Сей бесполезное, бренное, дикое,
меж васильков и лилей
по циферблату надмирному тикая, —
время справлять юбилей:
ты расчесаться по этому случаю,
преобразиться должна.

Время с грехами, какими бы ни были,
ушестерившими прыть,
разом расстаться, — достаточно прибыли,
чтобы расходы покрыть;
будет возмездие, благополучию
только на пользу война.

Солнце ослепло, Луна отоварена,
звездам залеплены рты, —

* * *

The son of Providence, trusting his budget,
said unto us: I augur the hour of the comet.
Count Khvostov

Vindictive goddess, statue now woken,
 you're evil's bright herald!
What more do you foretell, tailed one?
 What else has that tail carried?
What is—of famine, misfortune, sorrow—
 your most irresistible menace?

Ice floe, frigid in Heraclitan flames:
 his irreconcilable struggle!
Go out doubt-free, and feel no shame—
 sow coffins into the hibernal
earth, while a weedy sward grows
 shoots for mole-crickets and den mice.

Sow what's useless, maddening, absurdist,
 between cornflowers and lily,
upon that clockface, ticking pendulous
 over the world. It's time to mark our jubilee.
And please comb your hair for this event.
 You're obliged to be transformed.

It's time to put sin aside, for though it
 sextuples our vigor,
it should now be cut off—we've profit
 enough to satisfy creditors.
Recompense gluts the pockets
 of the prosperous; war is our gain.

The sun's sightless, the moon's couponed;
 starlight's tight lips have crusted shut.

гостем непрошеным — хуже татарина —
    вдруг заявляешься ты
непринужденному званому ужину
    новый придать оборот.

Не разражаясь торжественной одою,
    как устоять в стороне? —
Весь поэтический жар израсходую,
    на год отмеренный мне:
переливающуюся жемчужину,
    вынув, Господь уберет.

Послана миру десницею Божьего,
    прямо с постели, босой,
без покрывала, с прозрачною кожею,
    с длинной-предлинной косой,
большеголовая рыжая девочка,
    чтобы ответить за всё.

1997

And like an uninvited guest—worse than
    a Tatar—you suddenly turn up
at this belly-laughing, black-tie banquet
    to unloose a new turn.

How, without breaking into Pindaric odes,
    can I stand by on the sidelines?
I'd blow my poetry's fiery load
    on the few years I'm resigned
to. Having removed this pearl—iridescent,
    smooth—God gathers it in.

Earthbound from God's elderhand
    and barefooting straight from bed—
with no shawl to veil such lucid
    skin—a red-head sails, her girlish braid
trailing from her head—
    she'll answer for everything.

1997

NOTES

A poet deeply invested in his country's literary history and keen to explore his language as it morphs, Maxim Amelin is as erudite as he is eclectic. "It's interesting for me to experiment with the Russian language, with its latent possibilities," he writes, "and that's why I work in the confluence of the 18th century and the present day." His poems, in short, strive to replenish his culture's literary stock by returning to its roots (Gavriil Derzhavin) and resurrecting its neglected writers (Vasily Trediakovsky, Count Dmitry Khvostov). Thus Amelin's interest in Nikolay Fedorov's 19th-century theory, "The Philosophy of the Common Task," which posits the perfectability of humanity and universal resurrection of the flesh. As Amelin notes, his poetry is Fedorovian—it resurrects and reanimates writers long gone.

Our notes attempt to clarify Amelin's literary resurrections and provide context to English-language readers. For reasons of space, such notes are just a sampling of the directions that Amelin's poetry can take readers willing to get lost in books. For further information on Amelin's tropes and themes, see our 2014 interview with him in *Jacket2*: "Resisting the Art of Entropy Triumphant" (online).

"Why repeat ourselves? More than was called": the italicized line in the Russian is taken from "Spring Warmth," a 1756 ode by Vasily Trediakovsky (1703–1768).

"In August the stars shoot through the night air": Numerous Russophone poets have paid tribute to the month of August, including Anna Akhmatova, Bella Akhmadulina, Joseph Brodsky, Nikolay Zabolotsky, Boris Pasternak, and Marina Tsvetaeva. Pushkin's famously productive autumn at his familial estate, Boldino—which actually began in September, not August—further contributes to this poem's context. Maxim Amelin was born on January 7, 1970: Christmas Day in the old, pre-revolutionary calendar.

"I'm thirty but feel three hundred": "Tripping over the same rake" is an idiomatic Russian expression for making the same mistake repeatedly.

Classical Ode to V. V. Mayakovsky: In Soviet times, the statue of Mayakovsky in downtown Moscow was a central locus for unsanctioned activity, both personal and political. The poem opens with two Soviet-style portmanteaus: Земшар and гертруды, translated here as "Globosphere" and "hero-works." Velimir Khlebnikov (1885–1932) called Mayakovsky the "Chairman of the World." According to Amelin, the emigre poet Georgy Ivanov ("Georges" in French, 1894–1958) was Mayakovsky's opposite. The poem contrasts the two poets' differing attitudes toward lower creatures and comments, somewhat ironically, on each man's hypothetical response to Nietzsche. The closing stanza features several famous lines from Mayakovsky's work, including this image from his suicide note: "the ship of love has crashed against everyday life."

"Each and every day, save weekends and holidays": The thinker who questioned the status of poetry after Auschwitz is Theodor Adorno.

"Homer's been shredded to quotes for the billboards": The original poem refers to "little horns of breathing," the comma-like diacritics indicating rough and smooth breathing in Ancient Greek. Such marks do not appear in Modern Greek. The Golden Age is a loosely defined historical period contemporary with Pericles (fifth century BCE).

"Rising at morning from my graveside": The poem alludes to the folk practice of wrapping sickly newborns in bread dough and "baking" them back to life in a corner of the stove. It saved Gavriil Derzhavin (1743–1816), a founding father of Russian literature, who almost died at birth. The epigraph and last line refer to Isaiah 26:9; the Canticle of Isaiah, based on this Bible verse, is sung in Orthodox matins.

The Joyous Science: The poem is a mock epic chronicling the real and imagined exploits of Jacob Bruce (1669–1735), an astronomer, alchemist, and military strategist for Peter the Great. The descendant of a Scottish clan, Bruce is credited with establishing Russia's first observatory, writing its first geometry textbook, and publishing its first astronomical calendar. He helped Peter the Great (1672–1725) in his efforts to modernize Russia; he might best be understood as a Russian version of Benjamin Franklin.

The poem's fantastical turns allude to Bruce's rumored mastery of the dark arts. According to some, Bruce could make young men old and old men young. He also froze lakes in summer and attached human heads to iron birds. (The birds, it is said, would fly from his home in Sukharev Tower.) Such tall tales speak to the suspicion that the Enlightenment elicited in Russia. They also highlight the joy of innovation when innovation still seemed surreal. Like Bruce, Amelin is both prankster and reformer. Like Bruce, he leavens his rigor with mischief.

A few notes on references: "Dammit, I'm mad" is a palindrome that echoes similar wordplay in the Russian. Ivan Motorin (1660s–1735) made monastery church bells, but after the loss of artillery at the Battle of Narva (1701), Peter the Great ordered Motorin to produce canons instead. "Falconet's grim statue" refers to the Bronze Horseman, a statue of Peter the Great in St. Petersburg, commissioned by Catherine the Great and sculpted by the Frenchman Etienne Maurice Falconet. The statue depicts Peter astride a horse that's trampling a snake (referred to later in the poem). The Thunderstone is the enormous rock serving as the statue's pediment.

Our chosen line—we translate into a loose ballad meter—is shorter than Amelin's original, as explained in the Introduction. Therefore, we added more stanzas.

On the Acquisition of a Volume of V. I. Maikov's Works and Translations: Baron Vasily Ivanovich Maikov (1728–1778), a coeval of Lomonosov, Sumarokov, Kheraskov, and other prominent

18th-century men of letters, was highly regarded during his lifetime for his odes and mock-heroic epics, but later fell from the canon. The poem gestures to an incident when the young Derzhavin was sent to Maikov's on an errand and lingered outside the famous man's sitting room, eavesdropping spellbound while the grand figures of literature read their work aloud.

"You take root in earth; I trot blithely by": In the gospels of Mark and Matthew, Christ curses a barren fig tree, which then withers. The walnut tree figures in the poem "Nux," dubiously attributed to Ovid, where the tree complains that any passers-by can pelt it with stones. (This is thought to reflect Ovid's plight in exile.) In both cases, a tree suffers unjustly. Amelin's original refers only to fig trees, an error that stems from a Russian mistranslation of Ovid.

"Temple with an Arcade": The title is a quotation from a Russian travel guide.

Katabasia for St. Thomas Week: The word "katabasia" refers to hymns sung in Russian Orthodox churches; the descent into the underworld (such as in book 11 of the *Odyessey*); and Russian slang for "confusion" or "a muddle." The poem imagines the awkward situation that would result if Fedorov's imagined resurrection took place. (For more on Fedorov, see the Introduction.)

The other figures mentioned in the poem are as follows: Count Dmitry Khvostov (1757–1835) was a prolific poet, prone to overblown rhetoric, and regarded by many as a graphomaniac. Pushkin mocked him in epigrams. Amelin wrote a recuperative forward to a 1997 collection of Khvostov's work. The poet Afanasy Fet's real last name was Shenshin (1820–1892). The initials F. I. T. belong to the poet Fedor Tyutchev (1803–1873). Both Tyutchev and Fet are regarded as among the greatest of Russian lyric poets. (In 1866, Tyutchev famously described Russia as something that can't be understood intellectually—you have to have faith in it.) In "It Happened by the Sea," the poet Igor Severyanin (1887–1941) describes a tempestuous night of love between a queen and her page; "Severyanin's page-boy" became a Silver Age commonplace.

Belated Ode to Catherine the Great: Those whose images accompany the Empress are, in order of appearance: Fleet Commander Vasily Chichagov, who led the Russian navy during the Russo-Swedish War ("undrowned by Swedish sailors"); Field-Marshal Petr Rumyantsev-Zadunaysky, who led the Russians to victory in several battles of the Russo-Turkish War ("snapped the Turkish crescent's horns"); General Aleksandr Suvorov, arguably the best military leader in Russian history ("plucked the feathers off state birds"); Chancellor Aleksandr Bezborodko, architect of Catherine's foreign policy ("made a needed peace"); Count Aleksey Orlov-Chesmenskiy, who served Catherine in her political intrigues as much as in his successful naval battles ("conquered salty puddles"); Prince Grigory Potemkin, Catherine's right-hand man and erstwhile lover, whose efforts led to the annexation of Crimea and to Russian victory in the second Russo-Turkish War ("victor both of battles / and of bedsheets"); Ivan Betskoy, President of the Russian Academy of Sciences and founder of the Smolny Institute, the first educational establishment for women in Russia (taught the "young, strong river"); Princess Yekaterina Dashkova, the brilliant confidante whom Catherine appointed Director of the Russian Academy of Sciences and President of the Russian Academy, and who was also the first woman invited to join the American Philosophical Society, by its most famous co-founder, Benjamin Franklin ("bred herds of thought"); and the poet Gavriil Derzhavin ("righteous herald of deeds").

"The lilac has faded, the jasmine's begun to bloom": "Little Nikitskaya and Bronnaya avenues" are streets in a pleasant central Moscow neighborhood.

"Vindictive goddess, statue now woken": "Sow what's useless, maddening, absurd" plays on a famous line from Nikolay Nekrasov's "To the Sowers" (1876): "sow what's sensible, good, eternal."

ACKNOWLEDGEMENTS

Asymptote: "I'm thirty but feel three-hundred," "Long now you've lounged in earth—futile," and "Rising at morning from my graveside"; *Atlanta Review*: "Homer's been shredded to quotes for the billboards" and "Temple with an Arcade"; *Big Bridge Magazine: An Anthology of Twenty-First Century Russian Poetry* (online): "I'm both enraptured and indignant"; *Cardinal Points*: "Belated Ode to Catherine the Great" and "Dawn's rosy advent reddened the east"; *Cerise Press*: "Where burdocks and nettles" and "On the Acquisition of a Volume of V. I. Maikov's Works and Translations"; *Chtenia: Readings from Russia*: "There's no peace on earth or in heaven"; *Circumference*: "Katabasia for St. Thomas Week"; *Gobshite Quarterly*: "Cyclopean language consists of consonants"; *International Poetry Review*: "Foray into Patriotism," "Inscription over the Entrance to a Tbilisi Banya," and "Wasn't I the man who seized"; *Jacket2*: "Temple with an Arcade," "Vindictive goddess, statue now woken" and "Why repeat ourselves? More than was called"; *Lunch Ticket* (online): "The language of Aesop eludes me," "Each and every day, save weekends and holidays," "In Memory of East Prussia," "A many-throated, many-mawed rumble," and "You take root in earth; I trot blithely by"; *Mantis:* "Harder than hard and simpler than simple" and "The lilac has faded, the jasmine's begun to bloom"; *Reunion: The Dallas Review*: "Teach me to beseech you, O Lord," "In August the stars shoot through the night air," "I wish I owned my own home," and "The hulking carcass of a dead orca"; *Two Lines*: "Classical Ode to V. V. Mayakovsky" and "Fire-breathing beast, fumes wreathing your figure"; *Waxwings*: "The Scribe's Confession"; *World Literature Today*: "Let's hurry," "Satiety prevails, not taste," "These nights that won't wear out in July," and "The Statue of Silenus in the Capitoline Museum in Rome."

"The Joyous Science" first appeared, in its entirety, in the *Brooklyn Rail* in April of 2016. The poems appearing in *Lunch Ticket* were semi-finalists for The Gabo Prize for Literature in Translation & Multi-Lingual Texts (2014). "The lilac has faded, the jasmine's begun to bloom" also appeared in the Russian bilingual anthology *100 Poems about Moscow* (ed. Artyom Skvortsov). On June 6, 2017, six of these translations appeared in *Russia Beyond the Headlines* (online). Thanks to all the editors who published our translations over the years.

We'd also like to express our gratitude to the following individuals who—through conferences, reading invitations, interviews, editorial guidance, friendship, or some combination therein—helped bring Amelin's poems the attention they deserve: Alex Cigale, Sibelan Forrester, Peter Golub, Nicole Monnier, and Katerina Stoykova-Klemer. Thanks to Bronwen Wickkiser for a last-minute assist with Greek. Anne requested help from many knowledgeable people regarding subtle or difficult passages; any mistakes in the final product are our own. We are grateful to Mikhail Viesel for introducing us to Amelin. Thanks as well to Wabash College, whose Byron K. Trippet research fund helped to support our cover design, and to Robin Vuchnich for designing that cover. Thanks to the American Literary Translators Association for their Cliff Becker Translation Prize. Thanks to Maxim Amelin for his friendship, his assistance, and his poems.

A special thanks is due to Robert and Jean Mong, whose gift of childcare allowed us to finish the long poem at the center of this book. Finally, we are indebted to the National Endowment for the Arts for supporting our work on Maxim Amelin's poetry with a 2010 Literature Fellowship in Translation.

BIOGRAPHIES

Maxim Amelin is a poet, critic, translator, and publisher who graduated from the Commercial College in Kursk, served in the Soviet Army, and studied at the Gorky Literary Institute in Moscow. He has published three books of poetry—*Cold Odes* (*Холодные оды*, 1996), *Dubia* (1999), and *The Horse of the Gorgon* (*Конь Горгоны*, 2003)—and numerous articles and essays. His selected works, *Bent Speech* (*Гнутая речь*) appeared in 2011. His translations from Greek and Latin classics (Pindar, Catullus, the *Carmina Priapea*) as well as contemporary Georgian, Italian, Ukrainian, and other poets, constitute another sizeable oeuvre. As an editor, he has produced volumes of Russian and Georgian poetry from the 18th through the 20th century; he also edited the award-winning *Anthology of Contemporary Poetry of the Peoples of Russia* in 57 languages. His many awards include the Solzhenitsyn Prize (2013) and Russia's national award for poetry, the Poet Prize (2017). He is a member of the Russian PEN-Club and the Guild of Literary Translators and serves on the advisory board for the journal *Novyi Mir*. He lives in Moscow, where he is editor-in-chief of OGI Publishing House.

Derek Mong is the author of two poetry collections from Saturnalia Books, *Other Romes* (2011) and *The Identity Thief* (2018), and a chapbook, *The Ego and the Empiricist* (2017), which was a finalist for the Two Sylvias Press Chapbook Prize. A former poetry editor at *Mantis*, he is now the Byron K. Trippet Assistant Professor of English at Wabash College. He holds degrees from Stanford, the University of Michigan, and Denison University. His poetry, prose, and translations have appeared in the *Kenyon Review*, the *Southern Review*, *Blackbird, At Length, Pleiades, Two Lines, Poetry Northwest*, the *New England Review*, and the anthology, *Writers Resist: Hoosier Writers Unite* (2017). The recipient of awards from the University of Louisville, the University of Wisconsin, the *Missouri Review*, and Wolverine Farms, he now lives in Crawfordsville, Indiana. He and his wife, Anne O. Fisher, won the 2018 Cliff Becker Translation Prize for the *The Joyous Science.* They are the parents of a young son. Mong blogs at the *Kenyon Review Online* and reviews poetry for the *Gettysburg Review.*

Anne O. Fisher has translated three books by Ilf and Petrov: *The Twelve Chairs* (2011), *The Little Golden Calf* (2009), and *Ilf and Petrov's American Roadtrip* (2006). Her translation of Ksenia Buksha's novel *The Freedom Factory*, which received Russia's National Bestseller prize, is forthcoming from Phoneme Media in 2018. Most recently Fisher has translated Sigizmund Krzhizhanovsky, Nilufar Sharipova, Aleksey Lukyanov, and Julia Lukshina. Fisher has team-taught translation courses for Wabash College and the University of Wisconsin-Milwaukee. She has received grants from both the NEA and NEH, and her work has been recognized with a Northern California Book Award, the AATSEEL Prize for Best Literary Translation, the Rossica Prize, and—with husband Derek Mong—the Cliff Becker Prize. With Margarita Meklina, Fisher is editing and translating a folio of new Russian LGBTQ writing. She holds degrees from the University of Oklahoma and the University of Michigan and lives in Indiana.

The Cliff Becker Book Prize in Translation

> *"Translation is the medium through which American readers gain greater access to the world. By providing us with as direct a connection as possible to the individual voice of the author, translation provides a window into the heart of a culture."*
>
> —Cliff Becker, May 16, 2005

Cliff Becker (1964–2005) was the National Endowment for the Arts Literature Director from 1999 to 2005. He began his career at the NEA in 1992 as a literature specialist, was named Acting Director in 1997, and in 1999 became the NEA's Director of Literature.

The publication of this book of translation marks the culmination of work he had done in support of his personal passion for ensuring the arts are accessible to a wide audience and not completely subject to vagaries of the marketplace. During his tenure at the NEA, he expanded support for individual translators and led the development of the NEA Literature Translation Initiative. His efforts did not stop at the workplace, however. He carried out his passion in the kitchen as well as the board room. Cliff could often be seen at home relaxing in his favorite, worn-out, blue T-shirt, which read, "Art Saves Me!" He truly lived by this credo. To ensure that others got the chance to have their lives impacted by uncensored art, Cliff had hoped to create a foundation to support the literary arts which would not be subject to political changes or fluctuations in patronage, but would be marked solely for the purpose of supporting artists, and in particular, the creation and distribution of art which might not otherwise be available. While he could not achieve this goal in his short life time, now, seven years after his untimely passing, his vision has become manifest.

In collaboration with White Pine Press and the Cliff Becker Endowment for the Literary Arts, the Creative Writing Program at the University of Missouri, together with his surviving wife and daughter, has launched an annual publication prize in translation in his memory. The Cliff Becker Book Prize in Translation will produce one volume of literary translation in English, annually, beginning in the fall of 2012. It is our hope that with on-going donations to help grow the Becker Endowment for the Literary Arts, important artists will continue to touch, and perhaps save, lives of those whom they reach through the window of translation.